Chapter 2: The basis for socialism is the St...
take away wh...

Chapter 3: You do not nee...
exercise a right ... need a permit
to exercise a privilege. Privileges may be taken
away at any time for any reason

Chapter 4: As Americans, we are Kings. We are sovereigns.
It's good to be King! We have a moral
obligation to overthrow an oppressive government.

Chapter 5: Forms of Government
A republic has greater protection of individual rights.
A democracy is two lions and a lamb deciding
what is for dinner.
Socialism is a stepping stone to communism
Communism is evil

Chapter 6: Ten planks of Communist Manifesto
We're closer to Communism than you think

Chapter 7: One nation made of fifty states or
fifty states united into one body?
What is proper role of state v. country

Bill of Rights
was compromise

Chapter 8: THE PREAMBLE
→ Introduction: Why are we writing this
constitution? → To secure the best government
and get it in writing. It's our contract.

Chapter 9: ARTICLE 1: LEGISLATIVE BRANCH
→ Great compromise between small & large states
→ Constitution essentially set forth the actions
later leading to abolition of slavery
→ Senators were not originally selected by people (17th amd.)
→ Only Congress has the power to declare
war

Chapter 10 -13: Branches of Government

Chapter 14: memorize the Bill of Rights!

Bill of Rights does not grant us rights. we already have them. the BOR records them.

Chapter 15: Freedom of speech, religion, assembly

Chapter 16: Freedom to keep & bear arms

Chapter 17: Pre-eminence of private over public property,

Chapter 18: Accusation of crime
- Common law
- Jury
- Bail, cruel/unusual punishment

Chapter 19: Paradox of recording rights v. not recording them

Bill of Rights/ Const. limits the powers of the Federal Government

Chapter 20: Slavery Question v. Titles

Chapter 21: IRS & Federal Reserve (1913)
Was the IRS' Income Tax Ratified?

Chapter 22: Making something illegal does not necessarily prevent it

Chapter 23: Various perspectives on money

Chapter 24: Real Money: Gold & Silver

In medieval Europe, only the King could own property.

While lands were often "granted" to nobles, or administered by over-seers who might be allowed a percentage of the profits, actual ownership remained exclusively in the hands of one man alone: the King.

When the colonists arrived in the New World, they brought a resentment of that exclusivity with them. When America won her freedom from Great Britain, our Founding Fathers established a nation where any man could own property and have his rights respected. In other words, a land where every man could be a king.

And so we discovered what royals knew from birth: It's good to be King!

This book was written for Everyman, just as our Constitution was written for us all. It's an easy-to-understand primer on the civics lessons we should have learned in high school but were never taught. This is your chance to find out what you've been missing and why, in America, you are the King.

? About common v. statutory laws

Wording of Patriot Act

Chapter 25: Corruption in the United States

1. Abraham Lincoln - Civil War
2. FDR - WWII? Depression
3. Clinton- Ruby Ridge, WACO, Okla. City

| our leaders are taking away our rights!

Chapter 26: What Can I do?
1. Vote 3rd Party
2. Use liberty dollar
3. Refuse to give up freedoms
4. FIJA
5. New Hampshire Free State
6. Texas Constitution 2000

GOOD *to be* KING

GOOD *to be* KING

The Foundation of Our Constitutional Freedom

MICHAEL BADNARIK

THE WRITERS' COLLECTIVE   Cranston, Rhode Island

Independent Books for Independent Readers

Book Jacket Design: Barbara Hodge
Book Jacket Copy: Lisa Grant
Interior Design: Mary Jo Zazueta

For an explanation of the title, read Chapter Four.

ISBN 1-59411-096-4

Library of Congress Control Number: 2004097055

Printed in the United States of America
10 9 8 7 6 5 4 3 2 1

Published by The Writers' Collective ▲ Cranston, Rhode Island

To my parents, John and Elaine Badnarik, who devoted their lives to raising my brothers and me to be good Americans, and who always taught us to be the very best we could be.

Contents

FOREWORD

Michael Badnarik has created a constitutional primer that will edify and entertain schoolchildren and seasoned libertarians alike. *Good to be King: The Foundation of Our Constitutional Freedom* presents a thoroughly readable explanation of how our constitutional republic should work, and how the system became broken in the first place.

Mr. Badnarik starts with fundamentals, identifying the difference between rights and privileges. He discusses the critical and needed distinction between republican and democratic systems of government, arguing that freedom can survive in America only if we return to our republican roots. He also illustrates the forgotten tenets of federalism and states' rights, arguing that federal usurpation of state power has accelerated the loss of our freedoms.

The author then provides a detailed explication of the true meaning of major constitutional provisions and amendments. He does an excellent job of demystifying our founding document, demonstrating that ordinary Americans can and should understand the Constitution and how it applies to their lives.

Anyone who believes in limited government—that is to say anyone who believes in liberty—will benefit from reading this book. If we wish to remain free, we must constantly question and challenge conventional views about the proper role of government in our society. *Good to Be King* will serve as needed ammunition for libertarians and constitutionalists committed to resisting tyranny in America. I commend Michael Badnarik for authoring a compelling text on the foundations of liberty in America.

CONGRESSMAN RON PAUL, R-Texas

PREFACE

"Give me liberty, or give me death." Most of us are familiar with this famous quote, however very few Americans understand how precious our freedom really is. What else could explain the fact that we allow our rights to be trampled without so much as a whimper? Our Founding Fathers would be disappointed with us, and justifiably so. Give me liberty or give me *death*? Most of us refuse to do as much as turn off the television! Fortunately, there is a growing awareness in America that something is not quite right, and perhaps even terribly wrong. The purpose of this book is to help you examine the "self-evident truths" that led to the ratification of the Constitution, so that you can ultimately understand its true purpose.

It is said that we fail to fully appreciate something until after we've lost it. If we allow our liberties to slip through our fingers, it is not likely that we will ever be able to reclaim them. I do not pretend to be the first American who is concerned about the loss of our liberties. Daniel Webster wrote:

"I apprehend no danger to our country from a foreign foe ... Our destruction, should it come at all, will be from another quarter. From the inattention of the people to the concerns of their government, from their carelessness and negligence, I must confess that I do apprehend some danger. I fear that they may place too implicit a confidence in their public servants, and fail properly to scrutinize their conduct; that in this way they may be made the dupes of designing men, and become the instruments of their own undoing. Make them intelligent, and they will be vigilant; give them the means of detecting the wrong, and they will apply the remedy." (June 1, 1837)[1]

I have decided that I will not sit idly by when our rights are being violated by the people we have chosen to defend them. I am determined to "make them intelligent" by raising public awareness in the Constitution and the Bill of Rights. How you choose to "apply the remedy" is completely up to you.

The fires of liberty must be lit one heart at a time until everyone shares in the responsibility of defending it. Dr. Benjamin Rush said: "[Education] is favourable (sic) to liberty. Freedom can only exist in the society of knowledge. Without learning, men are incapable of knowing their rights, and where learning is confined to a few people, liberty can neither be equal nor universal." (1786)[2]

Please consider this book an adventure to be experienced rather than a story about the past. I want you to view the Constitution as yours, not as some ancient relic left behind by a forgotten generation. I want you share the passions that fueled the American Revolution. I want you to join me in the "animating contest for freedom."[3]

GOOD *to be* KING

CHAPTER 1

Ignorance is Bliss—But It's Still Ignorance

Much of what you think you know about the United States is probably wrong. You probably know, or think you know, that the Declaration of Independence was signed on the Fourth of July, 1776. Although we annually celebrate the birth of our country on that date, the Declaration was only *approved* by the Continental Congress on the Fourth of July. The text was sent to the printer on the Fourth for duplication in typeface. Approximately 200 copies were made and distributed among the colonies.[1] Later a calligraphy version was created and signed for the first time on August 2. That is the copy currently on display in the National Archive.

I will concede that perhaps this is just a mere technicality. However, I'll bet you don't even know the name of the first president of the United States. If your answer is George Washington, you—like so many other Americans—have an incomplete grasp of our nation's history. We agree that the Declaration of Independence was signed in 1776, even if the actual date of the signing is in dispute. However history records that George Washington didn't begin his first term as president until 1789, shortly after the Constitution was ratified by the state conventions. That leaves the first thirteen years of our country's leadership unaccounted for. Did the colonies flounder aimlessly through the revolution with no one acting as the head of state? That would be very unlikely. Perhaps a document known as the Articles of Confederation will resurrect a distant memory from your casual brush with American history. The Articles of Confederation were the first "constitution" to define the scope of American government. During that time the united States (sic) chose a different president every year. The first president of the united States was a man named Samuel Huntington. Nine others were elected to that position before George Washington assumed the office.[2] In other words, George Washington is the first president of the United States under the Constitution, but he was the eleventh president of the United States. Therefore, your information wasn't completely wrong, but it wasn't completely right, either.

I apologize if this seems more like a practical joke than a history lesson. It is not my intention to make you feel ignorant, but rather to make you question what you *think* you know. I want to challenge your assumptions so you will consciously and deliberately analyze the ideas in this book. I am an iconoclast—a breaker or destroyer of images; one who attacks cherished beliefs and traditional institutions as being based on error or superstition.[3] I admit it proudly. I intend to rattle your cage, and perhaps make you mildly uncomfortable at times. I am willing to take that risk because I sincerely believe that the end result is worth the aggravation. I urge you to challenge conventional thinking. Don't take anything for granted. Figure things out for yourself. Always question authority—mine included.

Thomas Jefferson wrote: "We hold these truths to be self-evident ..." Today we might substitute the word "obvious" for "self-evident," however I contend that nothing is obvious. We must learn everything we know through experience and the relentless application of logic. It is obvious that the burner of a stove is hot—unless you are a toddler reaching up to see what mother is cooking. Even when she yells, "No! Hot!" the child will recoil because mother raised her voice, not because they comprehend the danger. Each of us has a long-forgotten memory stored deep in our subconscious that represents our first painful experience with blisters. After we've been burned, the concept of hot may be obvious, but not until then.

Thomas Jefferson makes the mistake of giving us too much credit. Like most people, he assumes that because he knows something, everyone else must know it too. Most Americans still wander through life with a childlike ignorance of what it feels like to be burned by tyranny. The value of life, liberty, and the pursuit of happiness is not likely to be obvious to us if we have never been victimized by the very government we created for the purpose of protecting those rights. Sadly, more and more people are feeling the sting of oppression as all three branches of government—legislative, executive, and judicial—usurp more power than the Constitution permits them to have.

Article I of the Constitution establishes the legislative branch, known to us as Congress. Shortly after the disaster of September 11, 2001, Congress rushed to pass the ill-named Patriot Act in a declared effort to protect us from terrorism. The Patriot Act is so unconstitutional that it will someday be recognized as blatantly subversive. The Fourth Amendment protects our privacy by requiring that all search warrants be issued only with probable cause, and supported by oath or affirmation. The Patriot Act presumes to supersede these requirements, allowing government agents to perform something called "sneak and peek" searches. That means that someone can enter your home to collect information by taking photographs or copying the contents of your computer's hard drive. They can then leave undetected, with no obligation to inform you of their visit for ninety days. If you think those agencies are likely to tell you about it after their three-month grace period, you are hopelessly naïve.

The Patriot Act also makes a mockery of the Sixth Amendment, which protects your right to a speedy and public trial, and your right to the assistance of counsel for your defense. Under the Patriot Act, government officials can simply label someone a terrorist, and then put them in jail indefinitely without an indictment, denying them the opportunity to make a phone call to notify friends and loved ones, or to obtain legal assistance to challenge the charges and establish their defense. The government assures us that this policy only applies to terrorists, however these individuals are not officially terrorists until they have been convicted of those crimes in a lawful court.

Before the United States was created, kings or emperors dominated the governments of the world. Those monarchs created new laws simply by writing them on paper and affixing their official seals. Our ancestors came to the new world and created what is generally considered (by Americans, at least) to be a much better form of government. Our Constitution is designed with of separation of powers. Article II of the Constitution establishes the executive branch, led by the president of the United States, whose powers are limited to executing the laws created by the legislative branch. Ever since Abraham Lincoln, however, American presidents have found it more convenient to sign executive orders that presume to make laws that apply to all American citizens. How does that differ from the kings and emperors who assumed dictatorial power over the territory under their command? Unfortunately, it doesn't—meaning that most of the men who have held that office in recent history are guilty of violating the Constitution.[4]

Article III of the Constitution establishes the judicial branch of government including the Supreme Court and other inferior courts. The Supreme Court has the responsibility of striking down any federal law that violates the Constitution, thereby providing another one of the checks and balances that were deliberately incorporated into our system of government. Franklin Delano Roosevelt requested that Congress pass several pieces of legislation as part of his plan to recover from the Great Depression. The Supreme Court repeatedly struck down the new laws as unconstitutional, frustrating FDR's plans. In retaliation, the president threatened to pack the court with a majority of liberal judges. This is possible because Article III doesn't specify how many judges will be on the Supreme Court, only that the president is the one who will appoint them. (The number of justices fluctuated quite a bit until 1870 when the number stabilized at nine.)[5] When Congress proposed the same laws a second time, the Supreme Court now timidly approved the legislation, reversing their interpretation of the Constitution to be friendlier to Roosevelt's demands. Those laws are collectively known as the "New Deal," however I refer to them the "Raw Deal."

In the off chance that I have been too subtle, allow me to clarify my position for you. I am explicitly accusing all three branches of our government of violating the Constitution. That is a harsh indictment, and one that will be pooh-poohed by all of the talking heads in the national media. My only reason for omitting members of the media from my accusations is because they are not regulated by the Constitution and they may exercise freedom of the press. Personally, I think the media do whatever the federal government wants them to do, making it utterly useless in the defense of liberty. If this book gains some popularity, it is quite possible that I will be labeled a terrorist and quietly shuffled off to a distant gulag somewhere. That is precisely the response that Joseph Stalin would have advocated, and the reason why I feel compelled to write this book while I still can.

You may, of course, disagree with my positions, but there should be no doubt where I stand on any given issue. All I ask is that you read my book with an open mind. Most of the preliminary topics should be "self-evident" and should resonate with all Americans, regardless of their political affiliation. As your understanding of the Constitution grows, your feelings towards the status quo are likely to change dramatically.

CHAPTER 2

Rights vs. Privileges

The most important concept in this book is the difference between rights and privileges. For that reason, this chapter can be downloaded from my web site at no charge, and may be reproduced and distributed without written permission, as long as it is copied intact and without modification.[1] A right is defined by *Black's Law Dictionary* as "a power, privilege, (sic) faculty, or demand, inherent in one person and incident upon another ... the powers of free action."[2] Please note that rights are "inherent" in a person. This means that it is physically impossible for rights to be extracted from a person by any means.

Imagine a brick made of lead. The first thing that will cross your mind is that this object will be heavy. Extremely high density or weight is an *inherent* quality of lead. If an object isn't heavy, you can be certain that it's not made of lead. You cannot put a lead brick into a vacuum and "suck out the heavy." You cannot put a lead brick into a microwave and zap it until it becomes light and fluffy. The quality of being heavy is one of the distinguishing attributes of lead.

Now recall some of the dreams that you've had. You can't put the unpleasant ones into a bag and bury them in the back yard. You can share your dreams with others, but you don't have to worry that someone will steal them from you when you're not looking. Your dreams are an *inherent* part of who you are. No one can extract your dreams from you. The same thing is true about your rights. When you die, your dreams will die with you. If someone kills you, they will deprive you of life, but they can never deprive you of your right to life.

I define a right as something you can do without asking for permission. The opposite of a right, therefore, is something you cannot do without asking for permission. Any time you need permission to do something it is a privilege. *Black's Law Dictionary* defines this as "a particular and peculiar benefit or advantage enjoyed by a person, company, or class, beyond the common advantages of other citizens. An exceptional or extraordinary power or exemption."[3] Rights and privileges are opposites. I have three corollaries to the definition of rights. They are:

- All rights are derived from property;
- Every right implies a responsibility; and
- The only limitation on your rights is the equal rights of others.

Let me demonstrate the principle behind my first corollary with an example. Suppose I walk out of my house onto my land. I can walk back and forth, back and forth, across my land anytime I want without asking anyone's permission. Walking across my land is a right. Now suppose I want to walk to the store located on the other side of your land. Can I walk back and forth across your land anytime I want to? Certainly not. Not without your permission. It is a privilege to walk across your land. Assuming that we've been neighbors for a while, it is possible that your response would be, "Sure you can take the shortcut, Mike. What are friends for?" So on Monday, Tuesday, and Wednesday I walk to the store making my way across your land. Let us now assume that something unpleasant happens to you. You misplace a winning lottery ticket, or your significant other leaves you for your best friend. You wake up Thursday morning in a terrible mood, looking for an opportunity to vent your frustrations. As I begin to make my way across your land you shout, "Hey, mister! Walk around! That's what fences are for!"

The important concept here is that privileges are granted, and they can be revoked at any time for any reason. Once again, rights and privileges are opposites.

Property! This is the one-word answer to any question regarding the Constitution. Any time there is a dispute about rights, the argument can be settled by determining who owns the property in question. Prior to the American Revolution, a man born into the proper family was thought to possess all of the land in England, and he claimed all rights as well. The king could bestow privileges on the people he favored and, being the king, he could revoke those privileges at any time. He could also have a person sentenced to death for any action he found insulting. All his power came from his ownership of property. When Christopher Columbus marched out of the water onto a beach in North America, he immediately proclaimed ownership of the entire continent for Queen Isabella of Spain. Subsequent settlers would each declare ownership of the land for the royalty they felt they owed allegiance to. The king's power and prestige was directly related to how much land he possessed—which explains why human history consists almost exclusively of continuous warfare.

The Declaration of Independence states "they are endowed by their creator with certain unalienable rights." This statement refutes the idea that only the king had any rights. Instead of accepting privileges controlled by a human king, we claim the same rights that every king has ever claimed. We consider this to be "self-evident" now, but it was necessary for us to defend this idea by fighting a bloody revolution that ended with the Treaty of Paris in 1783. The significance of this treaty was to transfer ownership of the land from the king to the people in America. Hence, the American Revolution was ultimately about the right to own property. The ownership of property is the most important distinction between freedom and tyranny. This idea is so important that John Adams, the twelfth president (right after George Washington) wrote: "The moment the idea is admitted into society that property is not as sacred as the law of God, and that there is not a force of law and public justice to protect it, anarchy and tyranny commence."[4]

Regardless of your religious views, I think it can be safely said that anything as sacred as the law of God would hold considerable weight in any argument. Unfortunately, not everyone in America holds property is such high regard.

Most of our problems in the United States can be traced to a blatant disregard for private property. Examine the quote of another American president, Theodore Roosevelt: "Every man holds his property subject to the general right of the community to regulate its use to whatever degree the public welfare may require it."[5]

If I own a piece of property, I control what happens to it. If the community has the "right" to regulate my property whenever it wishes, then I do not truly own the property. I am merely occupying it through the generous will of the majority. Both statements cannot be true at the same time.

This is a very simple concept understood by every two-year-old. Every two-year-old has two favorite words. Both are attempts to express their will over their environment. The first word is "no!" which is the equivalent of a royal veto—an attempt to forbid mother from doing something we don't approve of. This statement is rarely a *successful* veto, but it is uttered with the same assumption of autonomy as any king who ever lived. Their other favorite word is "mine!" frequently shouted with a presumption of unquestioned authority, regardless of the item being claimed. The child claims ownership of any item they wish to have control over. They already understand that if it is "mine!" then I am the one who will determine what happens to the item. In other words, "I have the right to do what I want with it." Of course children have an incomplete understanding of property, having a much more difficult time with the concept of "yours." Parents spend countless hours trying to teach their offspring not to touch other children's toys unless they are given permission. The problem does not go away in later years, either. Siblings sharing the same room will often draw a line down the center of the room to establish "ownership" and control over a given area and the property that it contains.

Adults assume that they have a much better understanding of property than children do, but that is not necessarily the case. Americans do not legally own property in the manner that they believe they do, because they do not exercise autonomous control over their property. What would happen if you erected a derrick in your backyard and started drilling for oil? Would you be surprised if the county sheriff drove up and asked to see your permit? In order to drill for oil you must own the property under "allodial title." Unfortunately, if you pay property taxes, then you do not own your property to the degree that you thought you did.

It may surprise many of you to learn that the federal government claims ownership of much of the land in each of the states, especially in the western states.[6] Much of the rest is claimed by the states themselves. This is clearly an important topic, unfortunately not one that I have time to explore rigorously here.

You probably don't own your car the way you think you do. If I give you a "gift certificate," do you have the gift, or just a piece of paper that represents that gift? When you finish making payments on your auto loan, does the bank send you the "title" to the car, or simply a "certificate of title"? The certificate of title is a piece of paper that only *represents* the title of the car. Each car that is manufactured has an MCO, or "manufacturer's certificate of origin," that is the true title for the car. Because most cars are purchased on a payment plan, the dealer sends the MCO to the state agency that controls the registration of vehicles. The MCO is microfilmed and then shredded to make it much more difficult for you to obtain the actual title. If you are able to pay cash for your car and you know enough to demand the MCO as part of the purchase agreement, it is possible for you to purchase an automobile and own it the way you currently believe that you own it. The figure on next page shows a copy of an MCO obtained by a patriot friend of mine. He is not required to register his car with the state, and he travels in it without license plates. All of this is perfectly legal—although you may admittedly have some difficulty convincing the police officer who has detained you for what appears to be a traffic violation.

Property may be an adequate source of rights for land, but what is the source of your right to life? Many will argue that your right to life comes from God, however that debate is outside the scope of this book. Whether divinely created or scientifically evolved, one thing that is indisputable is the fact that your body exists. It is also widely assumed, at least in the contemporary United States, that you own your own body. If someone else owns your body, then you are a slave. The institution of slavery was based on the premise that other humans were considered to be property, and thus could be bought and sold like any other commodity. That idea is loath to many of us now, however the Thirteenth Amendment prohibiting slavery and involuntary servitude was not passed until December of 1865. You cannot successfully claim your right to life until those around you respect your body as property that you alone con-

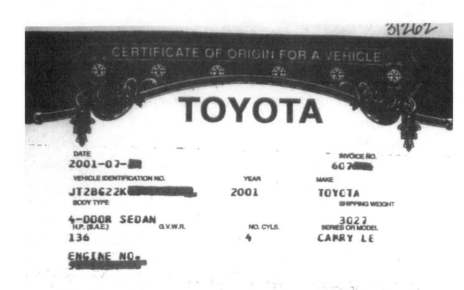

Copy of a Manufacturer's Certificate of Origin (MCO).

trol. Even today the women in Middle-Eastern countries are treated as the property of men, and children are still sold into slavery around the world.

The second corollary on the subject of rights is the fact that every right implies a responsibility. Rights and responsibilities are as inseparable as the heads and tails of the same coin. You cannot have one without the other. I have a right to wear a gun on my hip, but I also have the responsibility to make sure that no one is injured by it. Furthermore, carrying a gun does not give me a right to your property. I only have a right to my property, not to yours.

It is a widely held position that a six-year-old child has the right to life. I have never personally met anyone who has argued otherwise, but do not assume that this is a universal proposition. Does a six-year-old child also have the right to keep and bear arms? Very few of us—not even I—would allow a child to walk around with a loaded firearm. That's because a child does not have the mental capacity to grasp the possible consequences and implicit responsibilities of using a gun. To a child, everyone is immortal just like Wile E. Coyote in the Road Runner cartoons. A child thinks that if you fall off a cliff, there is a brief puff of dust and a few seconds later you're zipping along on rocket roller skates. Unfortunately, that type of rapid recovery isn't possible in the real world.

Americans have grown weary of their responsibilities, and our government has been only too eager to relieve us of those burdens. When two people have a child, they have a responsibility to determine what the child will learn and what values it should adopt. Over the years parents have become complacent about that responsibility, turning it over to government schools that offer "one size fits all" education. Then parents have the audacity to wonder why their children haven't adopted the values they would like them to have.

Instead of planning for their future, our parents and grandparents allowed the Socialist Insecurity Administration (sic) to take money from their paycheck to create their retirement program. Today, everyone is concerned that Social Security doesn't return enough money for basic subsistence, much less the money people need to enjoy their golden years. If people had retained that responsibility for themselves, placing their money in a simple savings account with 5 percent interest, they would easily have more money than they currently get from the government. By allowing the government to assume our responsibilities, we have gradually given away many of our rights.

My third corollary on the subject is that the only limitation on your rights is the equal rights of others. To put it another way, you only have the right to your property. You do not have the right to anyone else's property.

Many people believe that they have a right to health care. There is even a presidential candidate who recently suggested a constitutional amendment guaranteeing that right. A right to health care suggests that you should be able to walk into a doctor's office and insist that she or he correct your illness for free, or for a significantly reduced cost. Would you be willing to do your job for free for anyone who steps in off the sidewalk? I sincerely doubt it. You'd be very busy—and very, very poor. Why should your doctor provide services for free after spending all the time and money required to graduate from medical school? "Don't worry!" people tell me, "the government will pay the doctor's salary." Oh, really? And where does the government get the money to pay the doctor's salary? From taxes, of course. But for every $100 the government takes from my wallet, they keep $50, the HMO keeps $25, and the doctor gets what's left. Wouldn't it be easier and far more efficient for you to walk into my house to take $100 out of my wallet yourself? You'd be able to pay for even better treatment than you're getting right now. There is, of course, one small problem with that plan. I am a strong Second Amendment supporter. If you come into my house in an attempt to take money from my wallet, you will soon be going to the doctor for something far more serious than whatever you were suffering from in the first place.

You should have learned this in grade school, but just in case you missed it, you do not have a right to other people's property, not even when the government takes it away from them and gives it to you. That is the basis for socialism, and that is exactly what the Constitution is intended to prevent.

CHAPTER 3

Individual Rights

People are usually surprised to discover that I hate the phrase "constitutional rights." I hate that phrase because it is terribly misleading. Most of the people who say it or hear it have the impression that the Constitution "grants" them their rights. *Nothing could be further from the truth.* Strictly speaking it is the Bill of Rights that enumerates our rights, but none of our founding documents bestow anything on you at all. The Declaration of Independence was signed in 1776. Is that the first year Americans had the right to "life, liberty, and pursuit of happiness?" What rights did we have after the Constitution was ratified that we didn't have prior to 1789? Did the ratification of the Bill of Rights in 1791 create freedom of speech and freedom of religion for the very first time? All of those suggestions are obviously nonsense, but only after you've thought about them for a while. All of your rights precede these documents. The government can burn the Constitution and shred the Bill of Rights, but those actions wouldn't have the slightest effect on the rights you've always had.

The only type of rights that exist are individual rights. There is no other kind. Whenever I hear someone talk about "community rights" it is always in the context of suggesting that they somehow supersede individual rights. This is utter nonsense, however I will explain it just in case it isn't obvious to you. Individuals exist. You can reach out and touch an individual. Communities do not exist. They are abstract concepts that merely represent a collection of individuals. We do not start out with a large block of "community" and then shave off thin slivers of "individual." Communities do not (and cannot) have rights. Only the individuals within the community have rights, and those individuals continue to have rights whether they remain in the community or not.

The phrase community rights is always used as a justification for depriving one or more individuals of the rights they would ordinarily expect to have. The community has a right to live in a nice neighborhood, so the homeowners' association prevents you from painting your house pink, or leaving your boat in the driveway. The community has a right to a smoke-free environment so we force business owners to prohibit smoking in their establishments, thus violating not only the right of smokers, but also the rights of the business owners who *think* they own their property, but really don't.

Another phrase used to promote community rights is "the greatest good for the greatest number." Please note: This is the philosophical basis for communism. Let's take this policy to the inevitable extreme. You live in a community of twenty people, however there is only enough food for nineteen. It would be for the greater good of the community if one of the members was eliminated to prevent the remaining members from going hungry. Do you really believe that the majority can vote to put one of its members to death simply because they claim it is for the greater good? It is impossible to protect individual rights by claiming that community rights can supersede or nullify them. The only way to promote the good of the community is to unerringly protect the rights of the individual.

Liberty is often defined as the power of free action. One of the individual rights that you have is the unlimited right to contract. Here is an excerpt from a Supreme Court case known as Hale .vs. Henkel, 201 US 43 (1905):

"The individual may stand upon his constitutional rights as a citizen. He is entitled to carry on his own private business in his own way. *His power to contract is unlimited.* (emphasis, mine) He owes no duty to the State or to his neighbors to divulge his business, or to open his doors to an investigation, so far as it may tend to incriminate him. He owes no such duty to the State, since he receives nothing there-from, beyond the protection of his life and property. His rights are such as existed by the law of the land long antecedent to the organization of the State.... He owes nothing to the public so long as he does not trespass upon their rights."

The good news is that you have an unlimited right to contract. The bad news is that you have an unlimited right to contract. If I offer you $250 to "paint the house my dog sleeps in," you may consider that a fantastic opportunity. How big can a doghouse possibly be, anyway? After you sign the contract I can lead you to a thirty-room mansion explaining "This is the house my dog sleeps in." In this scenario you have been misled by a deliberate twist of wording, however that is possible with every contract that you sign—as well as other contracts that you didn't know you were agreeing to. More on that later when we talk about Article IV.

Any time the government allows us the privilege of doing something, it usually documents the fact by giving us a permit or a license. Examine these definitions from *Black's Law Dictionary*.

permit: To suffer, allow, consent, let; to give leave or license; to acquiesce, by failure to prevent, or to expressly assent or agree to the doing of an act.[1]

Notice that a permit *allows* you to do something that you could not do without permission.

license: A personal privilege to do some particular act or series of acts on land without possessing any estate or interest therein, and is ordinarily revocable at the will of the licensor and is not assignable.[2]

The key phrase here is "without possessing any estate or interest therein." If you are one of the property owners then you "possess estate therein" and you can perform the act or series of acts *without* a license. A license simply allows you to do what an owner can do without the license.

Let's examine an issue that most people take for granted. If you have a marriage license, what do you have permission to do now that you did not have permission to do before? More important, who gave you that permission, and where did that person or agency get the authority to give you permission in the first place? Did George Washington have a marriage license? (No.)

Did Thomas Jefferson have a marriage license? (No.) Did they simply ask the women they loved to settle down with them and perhaps raise a family? Remarkably—yes. This is one of the advantages of having an unlimited right to contract. What may be even more surprising to some is the fact that this is still being done today. Have you ever heard of a common-law marriage? Occasionally a couple will start living together without the formality of a ceremony. Generally the local busybodies will be all a-twitter because the pair is "living in sin," as if somehow the relationship is any of their business. So if the eleventh and thirteenth presidents of the United States (depending on where you start counting) didn't have a marriage license, then when (and why) was the very first marriage license issued?

Let's examine the status of blacks and whites during the middle 1800s. Can two white people decide to live together and make babies? Of course! White people have rights and can exercise their unlimited right to contract. Can two black people decide to live together and make babies? They certainly didn't have control over where they lived, so the fact that they had reproduced was viewed much like animal husbandry. If you owned the parents then your property inventory had simply increased by one. What if a black person and white person decided to live together and make babies? (Gasp!) Heaven forbid! The government certainly couldn't allow a mixing of the races, now could it? Here are some revealing definitions, again from *Black's Law Dictionary:*

marriage license: A license or permission granted by public authority to persons who intend to intermarry ...[3]

intermarriage: see miscegenation[4]

miscegenation: Mixture of races. Term formerly applied to marriage between persons of different races. Statutes prohibiting marriage between persons of different races have been held to be invalid as contrary to [the] equal protection clause of [the] Constitution. Loving v. Virginia 388 U.S. 1, 87 S.Ct. 1817, 18 1.Ed.2d 1010. [5]

Notice that statutes prohibiting interracial marriages are considered invalid, but that wasn't always the case. Keep in mind that white people had rights, whereas black people were only granted privileges. The white person could do just about anything they wanted; however, the black person had to get "permission" in the form of a "marriage license" in order to form a union with a white person. I'm guessing that a black person's chances of obtaining that permission were directly related to which white person they wanted to marry.

Just for the record, the "equal protection clause of [the] Constitution" can be found in Section 1 of the Fourteenth Amendment. Equal protection means that blacks and whites must now be treated the same. Did we grant blacks more freedom by eliminating the requirement to get "permission granted by public authority," or did we take away the rights of white people by requiring them to get a marriage license, too? "Equal protection under the law" apparently means that you can enslave blacks as long as whites are equally enslaved.

I hope it is now obvious that you do not require government permission in order to be married. (Common law marriages are valid in all fifty states, not because the government is benevolent and generous, but because common law is the highest law jurisdiction in America.) The government has no authority to tell me whom I can or cannot share a bed with, and I will adamantly ignore any statutes or laws that pretend otherwise. This is not a significant issue for me because I am heterosexual, however there are millions of homosexuals who are directly affected by the government's arrogant insistence that it will determine the definition of what constitutes a legal marriage. As far as I'm concerned, if you love someone and they love you back, you can exercise your unlimited right to contract with whomever you wish.

Let's up the ante a bit. If I have a right to keep and bear arms, then why must I get a concealed carry permit from the government? The answer is—I don't. Asking for permission to exercise a right is a contradiction in terms similar to a round square or a four-sided triangle. It is a concept that belongs in Alice's Wonderland. I will never accept permission from the government to exercise any right. It is simply un-American. For that reason I will never request a concealed carry permit. My rights are not negotiable. Many people think my views on the Second Amendment make me an extremist, however I prefer to think of myself as an absolutist.

If you are a mother with more than one child and I approach you with an offer to purchase one of them from you, would you be able to give me a price quote? Perhaps you have three children. I am only asking for one. I am even willing to take the one that you love the least. Are you willing to negotiate with me? No! Of course not! You're one of those extremist mothers who is so closed-minded that she won't even compromise. If you won't part with even one of your children, then you're an absolutist, too.

Let's assume you're a man who's married or has a steady girlfriend. I think I should be able to sleep with your significant other four nights a week. How many nights a week do you think I should spend with her? None? Come on! Won't you compromise with me? I'm willing to cut back to only two nights a week. I hope you're not one of those extremist boyfriends who thinks that you're the only one who deserves a little tender loving care. If you won't even let me take her out for dinner and a movie, then you too are an absolutist.

I have chosen these examples deliberately because I know they will evoke strong, visceral responses. I use them to demonstrate that there are certain issues that are absolutely not negotiable. There is no argument that can justify me purchasing one of your children, or sleeping with your spouse. The subject isn't open for debate—or at least it shouldn't be. The same thing is true about every discussion of rights. If your response to either of these situations was "over my dead body," then you finally understand the emotional basis for Patrick Henry's "give me liberty, or give me death" quote. Now contrast this position with those people who insist that we must give up some of our rights in order for the government to better ensure our security. These people may be misguided, but they are also dangerous, for they sincerely believe that people can justify taking away your rights if the majority votes in favor of the violation.

We cannot tolerate the government's assumption that we have to get a concealed carry permit in order to exercise our right to keep and bear arms. I know the thought of an armed society makes many people nervous, however the Second Amendment is just as non-negotiable as the First Amendment.

Have you filled out the government form that allows you to practice your religion? Certainly you don't want to be caught without the permit that allows you to go to church. I'm kidding, of course. You don't need a permit to go to church. At least, not yet. That's because your freedom of religion is protected (not granted) by the First Amendment. Our country was founded, in part, to protect a person's freedom of religion, and it will be one of the last freedoms that people will surrender—but surrender it they might. In communist Russia people were forbidden from practicing their religion as recently as 1980.

My mother visited Czechoslovakia shortly after the Iron Curtain was torn down, so she could explore our ancestral roots. During her visit she was invited to attend the first church services being held in public in more than fifty years. Needless to say those were very emotional events for everyone involved. The point is that you should never take your freedoms for granted, not even in the United States.

Do I seriously think that the American government would attempt to control our churches, or prevent us from exercising our freedom of religion? Most of the churches in America have already established themselves as 501-c3 tax-exempt organizations. Our current president strongly advocates faith-based charities, supposedly to assist in rebuilding family values. However every government handout comes with strings attached. Once the government has the power to refuse a tax exemption or deny faith-based funding, they will have the power to close selected churches by making them financially insolvent. The IRS has already closed down one church in Indiana because they refused to pay their taxes.[6] You probably don't have to worry, though. What are the chances that it will be your church that is shut down? Pretty slim, I'm sure, unless you are a Branch Davidian. But what if your church *is* shut down? What if the government finds some flimsy excuse to make your religion illegal? Would you break the law and hold your beliefs anyway? Would you attend secret underground services like they were doing in communist Russia? What would you be willing to do to prevent the possibility of having to even worry about this issue? Are you willing to fight to protect your freedom of religion? Are you willing to fight to protect the rights of others? When I was growing up my mother told me I only had to floss the teeth I wanted to keep. The same vivid lesson can be applied here. You only need to defend the rights you want to keep.

Patrick Henry is famous for his "give me liberty, or give me death" speech, but how far would you go to protect your rights? Most people don't give their driver's license a second thought. They have been told that driving is a privilege, and most people are happy to argue that we have to get a license; otherwise, the streets would be a dangerous place where accidents happen every day. This ignores the fact that the streets are a dangerous place and accidents do happen every day. Keep in mind that most accidents involve people who have a driver's license, so I'm not sure where the safety benefit is supposed to be. Let's take a closer look at the definition of license.

license: *Streets and highways* A permit to use [the] street is a mere license revocable at pleasure. The privilege of using the streets and highways by the operation thereon of motor carriers for hire can be acquired only by permission or license from the state or its political subdivisions.[7]

Notice that a license is "revocable at pleasure," meaning that it can be taken away at any time—but taken away by whom? Generally it is the owner who grants a license to do things on his or her property to people who could not otherwise do those acts or series of acts. Also interesting to note is that this particular privilege is granted to "motor carriers for hire," meaning someone who transports goods or passengers for money. Are you a motor carrier for hire? Do you earn a living by transporting goods or passengers? Is it possible that you are not legally required to have a "driver's license" unless you are a bus driver, cab driver, or truck driver?

I know that it will sound preposterous to most people, however the Criminal Court of Appeals of Texas, in a ruling known as Hassell v State (194 SW2d, 400), concluded that, "There being no such license as a 'drivers license' known to the law, it follows that the information, in charging the driving of a motor vehicle upon a public highway without such a license, charges no offense. Because of the defect in the information, the judgment is reversed and the prosecution ordered dismissed." For proof, see the figures at the end of the chapter.

One of the things I have learned is that legal definitions do not always mean what we may expect them to mean. Let's examine a few definitions related to driving. If a police officer pulls you over and gives you a ticket, the offense is one of thousands listed in the traffic code.

traffic: Commerce; trade; sale or exchange of merchandise, bills, money, and the like. The passing or exchange of goods or commodities from one person to another for an equivalent in goods or money.[8]

commerce: The exchange of goods, productions, or property of any kind; the buying, selling, and exchanging of articles. The transportation of persons and property by land, water and air.[9]

transportation: The movement of goods or persons from one place to another, by a carrier.[10]

carrier: Individual or organization engaged in transporting passengers or goods for hire.[11]

passenger: In general, a person who gives compensation to another for transportation. The word passenger has however various meanings, depending upon the circumstances under which and the context in which the word is used; sometimes it is construed in a restricted legal sense as referring to one who is being carried by another for hire; on other occasions, the word is interpreted as meaning any occupant of a vehicle other than the person operating it.[12]

vehicle: That in or on which persons, goods, etc. may be carried from one place to another, especially along the ground. [...] Term refers to every device in, upon or by which a person or property is or may be transported upon a highway.[13]

Based on these definitions, do you transport anyone or anything for hire? Is it possible that your automobile is a "personal conveyance" and not really a "vehicle'? Is it remotely possible that you are not legally required to have a "driver's license" unless you are a bus driver, cab driver, or truck driver? Think about it. I'm not asking you to throw away your driver's license. However if I've caused you to think seriously about some of the things you have previously taken for granted, you are well on your way to understanding the Constitution the way the Founding Fathers intended you to.

show system, and did not come within the exceptions allowing such proof.

[5] Bill of exceptions No. 3 complains because the State was allowed to ask appellant while he was on the witness stand the following question: "Haven't you been convicted of drunk driving in other counties adjoining Wise County?" It is true the witness answered "I don't remember," but in line with our holding as to bill No. 2 this question should not have been propounded to appellant.

On account of the error shown in bill No. 2, this judgment is reversed and the cause remanded.

HASSELL v. STATE.
No. 23353.

Court of Criminal Appeals of Texas.
May 15, 1946.

1. Automobiles ⚷137

Under Drivers' License Act it is unlawful for any person to drive or operate a motor vehicle over a highway of Texas without having a license, either as an operator, a commercial operator or a chauffeur, but one holding a license as a commercial operator or chauffeur is not required to have an operator's license. Vernon's Ann.Civ. St. art. 6687b, §§ 2, 3, 44.

2. Automobiles ⚷351

Information alleging that defendant operated a motor vehicle upon public highway without a "driver's license" charged no offense under Drivers' License Act, since a driver's license is not known to the law

Commissioners' Decision.

Appeal from Hunt County Court; Wm. C. Parker, Judge.

W. Lee Hassell was convicted of operating a motor vehicle upon a highway without a license, and he appeals.

Reversed and prosecution ordered dismissed.

G. C. Harris, of Greenville, for appellant.

Ernest S. Goens, State's Atty., of Austin, for the State.

DAVIDSON, Judge.

The conviction is for operating a motor vehicle upon a highway without a license; the punishment, a fine of $50.

By what is commonly referred to as the Drivers' License Act, and appearing as Art. 6687b of Vernon's Annotated Civil Statutes, the Legislature of this State provided for the licensing of operators of motor vehicles over the public highways of this State. Sec. 2 of Article II of the Act reads as follows:

"Drivers must have license.

"(a) No person, except those hereinafter expressly exempted, shall drive any motor vehicle upon a highway in this State unless such person has a valid license as an operator, a commercial operator, or a chauffeur under the provisions of this Act.

"(b) Any person holding a valid chauffeur's or commercial operator's license hereunder need not procure an operator's license.

"(c) No person holding an operator's, commercial operator's, or chauffeur's license duly issued under the provisions of this Act shall be required to obtain any license for the operation of a motor vehicle from any other State authority or department. Subsection (c) of Section 4 of Article 911A

Document from a Criminal Court of Appeals in Texas regarding driver's licenses.

"operator," a "commercial operator," or a "chauffeur." One holding a license as a "commercial operator" or "chauffeur" is not required to have an "operator's" license.

Certain exemptions and exceptions from the operation of the Act are provided in Sec. 3 of Art. II thereof.

The information upon which this conviction was predicated alleged that appellant "did then and there unlawfully operate a motor vehicle upon a public highway, to-wit, State Highway No. 24, without a Driver's License."

It is insisted that the information charges no offense, because a "driver's license" is neither recognized nor authorized to be issued under the Act and, by reason thereof, it constitutes no offense to drive a motor vehicle without such a license.

[2] Only three types of licenses are authorized or required under the Act. These are "operators," "commercial operators," and "chauffeurs," and they are specially defined in the Act. The term "driver"—as used in the Act—is defined to be: "Every person who drives or is in actual physical control of a vehicle." In view of this particular definition of the term "driver," it cannot be said that such term may be used interchangeably with or given the same meaning as the term "operator."

There being no such license as a "driver's" license known to the law, it follows that the information, in charging the driving of a motor vehicle upon a public highway without such a license, charges no offense.

Because of the defect in the information, the judgment is reversed and prosecution ordered dismissed.

PER CURIAM.

May 1, 1946.

Rehearing Denied May 22, 1946.

1. Habeas corpus ⬅4

An accused may not resort to habeas corpus as a substitute for an appeal.

2. Infants ⬅68

Any burden upon state to show in the first instance that accused was more than 17 years old, and thus not subject to the Juvenile Delinquency Act, was discharged when, upon hearing under his plea of guilty, accused testified that he was 17 years old and made the same statement in confession introduced in evidence. Vernon's Ann.Civ.St. art. 2338—1 §§ 12, 13.

3. Habeas corpus ⬅22(1)

Where accused stated in confession that he was 17 years old and testified to the same effect upon trial, no appeal was taken from conviction of felony theft on his plea of guilty, and judgment was regular on its face, accused was not entitled to release on habeas corpus on the ground that conviction was void because accused was only 15 years of age when convicted and could not be convicted of crime under the Juvenile Delinquency Act. Vernon's Ann.C.C.P. arts. 10a, 11; Vernon's Ann. Civ.St. art. 2338—1 §§ 12, 13.

On Motion for Rehearing.

4. Criminal law ⬅641(3)

The statutory requirement that, before a defendant who has no attorney can agree to waive a jury, the court must appoint an attorney to represent him, is mandatory. Vernon's Ann.C.C.P. art. 10a.

5. Criminal law ⬅982

The statutory requirement that when defendant has no counsel, the court must inform defendant of his right to make ap-

Document from a Criminal Court of Appeals in Texas regarding driver's licenses.

CHAPTER 4

Sovereignty

In times not as ancient as we might think, the prevailing theory of law was known as "the divine right of kings." Simply because he had won the lottery of birth, one man was assumed to be vested with all rights directly from God. The king owned the entire country as well as other lands around the world. Explorers would walk ashore on an uncharted land mass and immediately claim possession in the name of the king. For all intents and purposes, the king also owned everyone living in his country, and he had the right to delegate privileges to any of his subjects. One person would be the royal baker, another would be the royal candlestick maker ... until the king decided to take that privilege away. The king was sovereign.

sovereign: A person, body, or state in which independent and supreme authority is vested; a chief ruler with supreme power; a king or other ruler in a monarchy. [1]

Many English subjects relocated to the North American continent to settle. Eventually they grew tired of having their lives determined by someone else, and they wrote the king a nasty letter that we know as the Declaration of Independence. They had decided that, instead of getting privileges second-hand through the king, they would eliminate the middleman. They declared themselves to be sovereign citizens "endowed by their creator with certain unalienable rights." They were claiming the same status as any king or queen, including the right to own their own land.

We take land ownership for granted today, however in 1789 the concept was considered ludicrous. "No king? Who's going to make all the laws? The people? Ha!" This concept was so *revolutionary* that William Pitt found it necessary to address the House of Commons in England to explain it to the members of Parliament. He said: "The poorest man may, in his cottage, bid defiance to all the forces of the Crown. It may be frail; its roof may shake; the wind may blow through it; the storms may enter; the rain may enter; but the King of England cannot enter; all his forces dare not cross the threshold of the ruined tenement."[2]

This is where the expression, "A man's home is his castle" comes from. Imagine what would happen in England if someone were bold enough to "bid defiance to all the forces of the Crown." If you were lucky, you would be killed instantly. If you were not so lucky, the English had invented several different ways to make the pain of death excruciating. William Pitt explained that even the poorest man, not just the rich and powerful, can forbid the king from entering his home. "All his forces dare not cross the threshold of the ruined tenement." That's because now, even though it may be a tar paper shack, the king doesn't own it. Here is further evidence that property is absolutely essential for being able to assert your rights. You have the absolute authority to make all of the laws that affect any of the property you own. You are the king of your property, but I am the king of mine.

This means that the United States is occupied by nearly 285 million kings and queens. We are sovereign citizens, which means that we are the source of all political power. There is a maxim of law that predates the Magna Carta (signed in 1215) that claims the created can never be higher than the creator. We the people ... "ordain and establish the Constitution," and by doing so, we created Congress. If we created Congress, then who works for whom? Do we work for them, or do they work for us? The answer I get most often is, "Well ... they're *supposed* to work for us." Supposed to ... but they don't. Almost everyone these days has the nagging feeling that something is wrong with the way our government currently works, but they're not sure what it is. The purpose of this book is to explain how the government is *supposed to* work. I will leave it up to you to decide how we should change the way government *does* work.

Although you are theoretically sovereign and supposedly have absolute control over all of your property, the real world doesn't accurately reflect that fact. The reason that no one else considers you a sovereign is because you don't consider yourself to be sovereign. Why should other people give you more respect than you give yourself? Before we can change the way we think about government, we have to change the way we think about ourselves. You have to start by thinking that you're a king or queen, depending on your gender or preference. This exercise will probably make you feel very foolish the first few times you try it, but humor me and do it anyway.

When you finish this paragraph I want you to stand up tall, with your feet spread comfortably apart. Put your fists on your hips and take a deep breath. Then, with all of the authority and certainty you can muster, I want you to shout "It's good to be king!" You'll probably laugh the first time, but shout it again: "It's good to be king!" Look around you at all of your property. Know that you are the person who makes all of the decisions about that property. You are sovereign. No one can alter what you think. No one can supersede your authority. No one can (justifiably) violate the rights that were endowed to you by God. Once again then, with feeling! "It's good to be king!" Sure, your family will think you're nuts, but what else is new? If you practice this every day for a week, you will change the way you think about your relationship with the government. Go ahead and try this now. You'll thank me for it later.

Now that we've had a little fun, I want to get very serious for a moment. Unfortunately I feel it is necessary to make a short disclaimer due to the political atmosphere following the September 11 tragedy. I am not a terrorist. I do not advocate the use of violence to resolve problems, nor do I advocate the initiation of force against someone else. I would desperately like to be left alone, and I urge everyone else to do the same. However, I am perfectly content to use force to defend myself, my property, or my rights, if necessary, and I respect the right of others to protect themselves whenever they are being threatened.

What follows is intended to be a philosophical discussion, not an incentive to riot. I realize that this disclaimer will not stop John Ashcroft or his jackbooted thugs, but I thought I should at least make the effort.

I want you to think very seriously about the following question: If We the People are sovereign, do we have the authority to violently overthrow the government if necessary? Allow me to point out that there is no other way to overthrow a government, so the word violent is superfluous. There are no official forms you can fill out that will make the government shrivel up and go away. The Founding Fathers did not write a "Request for Independence" in 1776. It was a declaration, one that we had to enforce with seven years of bloody revolution. Let's analyze the question.

The Declaration of Independence is actually titled, "The unanimous Declaration of the thirteen united States of America" Note that united is in lower case since it is only used as an adjective. It says, "That to secure these rights, governments are instituted among men." This clause establishes the *only* valid purpose of government, which is to secure your rights. What happens when a government fails to protect your rights? "That when *any* form of government becomes destructive of these ends, it is the right of the people to alter or abolish it." So the Declaration explicitly states that we have a right to alter or abolish our government. What does the word abolish mean to you?

But the Declaration doesn't stop there. It says that, "Governments long established should not be changed for light or transient causes ... But when a long train of abuses and usurpations, pursuing invariably the same object, evinces a design to reduce them under absolute despotism, it is their right, it is their duty, to throw off such government, and to provide new guards for their future security." Please note that not only do you have a right to overthrow an oppressive government, you also have a moral obligation to do so. The same way that a parent has the responsibility of protecting a child, you have a responsibility for protecting yourself from your own government.

Thomas Jefferson is quoted as saying, "And what country can preserve its liberties if its rulers are not warned from time to time that this people preserve the spirit of resistance? Let them take arms! The tree of liberty must be refreshed from time to time with the blood of patriots and tyrants."[3]

Abraham Lincoln said, "This country, with its institutions, belongs to the people who inhabit it. Whenever they shall grow weary of the existing government, they can exercise their constitutional right of amending it, or their constitutional right to dismember or overthrow it."[4] He also said, "Our safety, our liberty, depends upon preserving the Constitution of the United States as our fathers made it inviolate. The people of the United States are the rightful masters of both Congress and the courts, not to overthrow the Constitution, but to overthrow the men who pervert the Constitution."[5]

I think that it is obvious that we *do* have the right to overthrow our government if and when we decide that it has become tyrannical. I often joke that my father used to tell me, "I brought you into this world, and I can take you out!" He never used those actual words, but there was never a doubt in my mind that he was in absolute control of the household. Similarly, We the People brought the Congress, the Office of President, and the Supreme Court into the world in 1789—and we can surely take them out again the moment we become aware of any violations of our Constitution.

It is difficult if not impossible to predict the future. It is much easier to look back through history using 20/20 hindsight. Hitler did not conquer Germany. He was elected to office with, in at least one instance, 98 percent of the vote.[6] He didn't begin the Jewish genocide the same week he was elected. It was a gradual process. He began by printing newspaper articles blaming the Jews for every social ill imaginable.

Did the Jews respond with newspaper articles of their own? Not that I'm aware of. Soon the Jews were being forced to wear the Star of David so they could be readily identified. Did they resist this blatant discrimination and refuse to comply with a violation of their privacy? No. How did they defend their freedom of religion? They "turned the other cheek" and adopted the attitude that they should be happy to wear the symbol to demonstrate their love for God.

Then on November 8 and November 9 of 1938, Nazi soldiers broke windows in 7,500 Jewish businesses during a weekend known as *Kristallnacht* or Crystal Night.[7] Did the Jews rise up in protest of this blatant persecution? Most did not. They didn't want to anger the Nazis any more than they already were. When the Nazis loaded the Jews into trains of cattle cars, where did they think they were going? On vacation?! When soldiers are leading you, naked and cold, toward the ovens where you will be executed *en masse*, is that the time to raise your hand and say, "Gee, I'm not really happy with this situation. Do you mind if we discuss it?" I'm sorry. It's too late for discussion. Oh, by the way. BANG! You're dead!

Looking back at the Holocaust it seems obvious to me that everyone, especially the German people, should have complained vociferously, long before World War II became necessary. I don't know if there will ever be a World

War III, but if there is, it will be because people waited too long to complain about their respective governments.

The American government is rapidly assuming more and more control over your life. The government continues to violate your rights on a daily basis, and still you refuse to resist. I have one final question for you in this chapter. It is a rhetorical question meaning that I don't expect you to send me your answer. I simply want you to ponder it within your own mind. The question is: How bad do things have to get before you will do something about it? Where is *your* line in the sand? If you don't enforce the constitutional limitations on your government very soon, you are likely to find out what World War III will be like. I'm quite sure that I will never experience that war—because dissidents are always the first to be eliminated.

CHAPTER 5

Forms of Government

George Washington said, "Government is not reason. Government is not eloquence. It is force. And, like fire, it is a dangerous servant and a fearful master."[1] Washington's metaphor suggests that, although we need some government, we must watch over it constantly so it doesn't get out of control. Government is the authorized use of force or power. In a dispute with your neighbor, you are not permitted to beat them with a baseball bat to resolve the issue. Instead, you call the police and let them deal with the problem. The assumption is that the police are less likely use excessive force because they remain emotionally detached from the situation. (Try telling that to Rodney King.) The most fundamental way to categorize different forms of government is to identify their source of political power.

A monarchy is a form of government where all of the political power resides in one person, such as a king or emperor.[2] We can refer to a monarchy as the *rule by one.* Those of us born with a stubborn, independent streak resent the idea of living under a dictatorship. However throughout human history, countless generations have quietly accepted the domination of such rulers as

Julius Caesar, Cleopatra, and King George III, without even questioning this monopoly of political power.

In other cases, the government may be led by a committee of several people, rather than relying on the benevolence of just one person. Such a government is called an oligarchy and can be referred to as *rule by the few*.[3] In other words, a small group of people make the laws, and everyone else is required to follow them. It is not surprising that laws made under these circumstances are strongly biased in favor of the few who are in power.

The Russian Politiburo is a recent example of an oligarchy. Because they were in control, members of the Politiburo lived in opulent luxury while the majority of the Russian population waited in line for hours in order to get loaves of bread and other government handouts. Given a choice, everyone would prefer to be a member of the group that makes the laws.

What if everybody could be a member of the group that makes the laws? There would be no disadvantaged group because everyone would share equally in the distribution of power. This form of government is called a democracy and is frequently known by the adage that *the majority wins*.[4] What is often overlooked in this equation is the fact that, if the majority wins, then the minority loses. So although everyone has an equal vote, society is still divided into competing factions of majority and minority—or to be more blatant, winners and losers.

If we apply the "majority wins" argument to every situation, the result is that rights do not exist in a democracy. That is because your "rights" can be voted away by a majority of the voters. If your "rights" can be voted away, then you only have privileges granted to you by the will of the majority.

Let's look at a contemporary example. Anti-gun activist Rosie O'Donnell helped organize a "Million Mom March" in Washington. The implied purpose of this movement was to get enough votes to eliminate the Second Amendment. While this goal was never explicitly stated, establishing new gun laws that successfully prohibit a person from keeping and bearing arms would amount to the same thing for all practical purposes. If you favor gun control, you should be aware that the same type of assault is being waged on First Amendment issues as well. There are currently heated debates on whether or not a statute of the Ten Commandments can or should be allowed to remain in the judicial building in Montgomery, Alabama. Both sides of this issue seem to feel that they will prevail if they can demonstrate a greater number of supporters. Anyone who supports the position that "this many people can't be wrong" will be frustrated by the fact that truth and rights are not determined by vote totals. If everyone in the room believes that two plus two is equal to five, then all of those people can be wrong.

Most people in the United States think that we live in a democracy. Those people are wrong. Our Founding Fathers were very familiar with history, and they knew the dangers inherent in a democracy. Alexander Fraser Tytler is quoted as saying:

> "A democracy cannot exist as a permanent form of government. It can only exist until the voters discover that they can vote themselves largesse from the public treasury. From that moment on, the majority always votes for the candidates promising the most benefits from the public treasury with the result that a democracy always collapses over loose fiscal policy, followed always by a dictatorship. The average age of the world's greatest civilizations has been 200 years."[5]

If the United States isn't a democracy, then what is it? Our first clue comes from the Pledge of Allegiance to the flag, "and to the republic for which it stands." A more authoritative reference can be found in Article IV, Section 4 of the Constitution, which reads, "The United States shall guarantee to every State in this Union, a Republican Form of Government."

So what is the difference, if any, between a democracy and a republic? I have heard many arguments that claim they are exactly the same thing, the first being a Roman word, the other having been derived from Greek. I'm not willing to accept this explanation because of the profound loathing the Founding Fathers seemed to have for democracy. They would not explicitly establish a republic if it were doomed to the same inevitable failure predicted for a democracy. Yes, both systems allow us to elect representatives. Yes, both systems allow the people to vote. The significant difference, as I see it, is that property and rights are not subject to a vote in a republic.

Assume that you and I are landowners, and that I have been attempting to purchase some of your land. Perhaps it has a supply of water that I would dearly love to have. You reject my offers for whatever reason suits you. At the next community meeting I make a proposal that will divide your land evenly between the other members of the community and myself. In a democracy, because "the majority rules," you could lose by a landslide, excuse the pun.

However, such a vote is completely meaningless in a republic, and has no force of law. In a republic, your land is your land. It cannot be taken away by the will of the majority. Therefore, in a republic, the rights and property of the minority are protected from the much stronger majority. To put it more simply, there are certain things you can't vote on in a republic. Rosie and her million moms are evidently unclear on this concept.

I've engaged in countless debates on whether or not there are significant differences between a democracy and a republic. A society can either vote away a person's property or it can't. I call the first situation a democracy, and the second option a republic. Those are the words I use to label these conditions. If you want to change the words around and play semantic games, feel free to do so. However if you try to take my guns or vote on the validity of my rights, you'd better bring a lunch because I plan to veto your conclusion.

If the only purpose for the Constitution is to protect your rights, and if you accept my thesis that all of your rights come from property, then it follows that the only purpose of the Constitution is to protect your property. The result of the American Revolution was that everyday citizens could now own property. Let's examine two forms of government where people are not allowed to own property.

socialism: A theory or system of social organization that advocates the vesting of the ownership and control of the means of production, capital, land, etc., in the community as a whole. It is significant to note that in Marxist theory *this is the stage following capitalism in the transition of a society to communism*, characterized by the imperfect implementation of collectivist principles.[6] (emphasis, mine)

Please notice that socialism is intended to be just a stepping stone in the plan to ultimately convert a country or nation to communism. It is "characterized by the imperfect implementation of collectivist principles." I guess we can assume that communism is the perfect implementation of collectives principles. So, what is communism?

communism: A theory or system of social organization based on the holding of all property in common, actual ownership being ascribed to the community as a whole or to the state.[7]

Please notice that all property is owned by the state, or government. In other words, *you* do not own your house. The government owns your house, and they just allow you to live there. It is not *your* car; it is the *government's* car. They are just allowing you to drive it until the government changes its mind. Let me take a quick survey. The first question: "In your opinion, is communism good or evil?" You probably found this to be an easy question. Assuming that you agree with most Americans that communism is evil, your second survey question is, "Why?" Because they fly a red flag? Because their soldiers march funny? Because your teacher told you so? Why do you think communism is evil? Perhaps you are one of those people who think that communism is fine in theory, however it has failed to work in practice. If you are one of these people, then you are only fooling yourself. Communism is evil in theory, and I intend to show you why.

CHAPTER 6

Communist Manifesto

In the mid-1800s, Karl Marx and Friedrich Engels were faced with the philosophical question of what the perfect communist state would look like. In other words, what conditions would be necessary to facilitate the "perfect implementation of collectivist principles"? The short essay they wrote has become one of the most famous written works of our world. Their thesis is known as *The Communist Manifesto*. It contains ten planks they felt were necessary in order to successfully achieve their goals. Here is a summary of those ten planks:

1. Abolition of private property
2. Heavy progressive income tax
3. Abolition of all rights of inheritance
4. Confiscation of property of all emigrants and rebels
5. Central bank
6. Government control of communication and transportation
7. Government ownership of factories and agriculture
8. Government control of labor
9. Corporate farms, regional planning
10. Government control of education

Please look carefully at the first plank, "abolition of private property." I've already asked you for your definition of "abolish" in a different context. How does that definition apply in this instance? Do you think that communists plan to allow some private property, or do you think it is their intention to deprive you of all ownership?

Do you recall the John Adams quote concerning property? It is: "The moment the idea is admitted into society that property is not as sacred as the law of God, and that there is not a force of law and public justice to protect it, anarchy and tyranny commence."

Clearly, if communists intend to abolish private property, they do not consider it "as sacred as the law of God." Without property, you have no rights. That is why communism is evil. A closer examination shows that the first plank describes what communism intends to do, and planks two through ten describe how they intend to do it.

Let's take a brief look at each plank. As you read, keep track of how many of these policies already exist in the United States. Keep a tally on a separate sheet of paper, or put a check mark along side each paragraph that describes an agency or policy here in the land of the free.

1. Abolition of private property

America's war on drugs has prompted government agencies to establish asset forfeiture laws which allow the arresting agency to take all of the property belonging to someone suspected of being involved with drugs. Frequently the arresting agency is acting on an anonymous phone call. The property is then sold at auction for a fraction of the cost, and the arresting agency keeps the money.

Whenever our government invokes eminent domain to take someone's property, they are demonstrating their lack of respect for private property, and acting just like any other communist regime.

2. Heavy progressive income tax

A progressive income tax means the more money you make, the higher your percentage of tax. In the United States the IRS determines the percentage of our progressive income tax. Those percentages are included as a table with the instructions that come with your 1040 form. If you make enough money, you may be lucky enough to fall in the 50 percent tax bracket. The strongest slaves are lucky enough to carry the heaviest rocks.

3. Abolition of all rights of inheritance

If your parents die without a will, the government may take half of everything your parents owned before you and your siblings are allowed to divide what's left. Even with a will the government can take a percentage. This prevents future generations within a family from accumulating a significant amount of wealth. What justifies this tax on dying?

4. Confiscation of property of all emigrants and rebels

Anyone who travels internationally must declare whether he or she is carrying more than $10,000 in money, stocks, or bank notes. Friends of mine who intend to relocate to New Zealand have been told that they cannot take their money with them.

5. Central bank

The Federal Reserve Bank is a private company and not a part of the American government any more than Federal Express is a part of the U.S. Post Office. You can prove this for yourself by searching the blue government pages in the phone book. When you fail to find it there, try looking in the white business pages. When you control the printing of money, it doesn't matter who controls the government. The Federal Reserve Act of 1913 is completely, totally, and unquestionably unconstitutional.

6. Government control of communication and transportation

The Federal Communications Commission controls all radio and television signals in the United States. The Federal Aviation Administration, National Transportation Safety Board, and every state department of transportation and motor vehicles control every aspect of transportation in this country. You cannot travel, ship, or broadcast anywhere in the United States without getting government approval.

7. Government ownership of factories and agriculture

Government doesn't actually own factories, but it also has no business bailing out Chrysler and savings and loan associations when they get into financial trouble. The recent collapses of Enron and WorldCom have suggested inappropriate connections with the government. The U.S. Department of Agriculture controls and regulates nearly every aspect of the food chain, from farm to table.

8. Government control of labor

Innumerable government agencies within the United States regulate nearly every facet of every kind of business. Although there is no formal government agency that directly controls unions, they are strongly influenced by federal agencies such as the Occupational Safety and Health Administration. (OSHA).

9. Corporate farms, regional planning

In the not-too-distant past, most farms were owned by small families. Now they are owned by large corporations and merely leased to the original tenants.

Every large city in the United States has a regional planning office. Austin, Texas, has a Planning and Design Office, a Planning/Environmental and Conservation Services Department, and a Planning and Economic Development office. Check your phone book to find similar agencies where you live.

10. Government control of education

There is no point in arguing whether or not the government controls education in this country. The Democrats and Republicans are falling all over themselves claiming to be the ones who control it best.

When the Department of Health, Education and Welfare (HEW) was established in 1953, American students ranked number one the world in the fields of math and science. Students from every other country were eager to come to the United States to get a good education. Eventually the Department of Education became a separate entity, but as of 2003 this country has experienced fifty years of government control of schools.

Statistics now rank American students as twenty-first in math and science. Our schools are now filled with children who can't read or write, and we spend ten times as much per student as we did in 1953. Even if the Department of Education was constitutional, which it is not, it should still be eliminated for doing such a terrible job.

So what was your total? Eight? Nine? Ten? I have always held that if it walks like a duck, and quacks like a duck, then it is probably a duck, regardless what the crowd around me is calling it. If the United States is already practicing all ten of these communist principles, then we must be living in a communist country. Does that give you a warm, cozy feeling inside, or are you suddenly concerned about the people in Washington who have promised to protect your rights?

CHAPTER 7

Our Founding Documents and Early History

Benjamin Franklin made a distinction between revolution and rebellion. The word revolution is an astronomical term that refers to the fact that a planet returns to where it started after a complete revolution. Franklin suggests that Americans were returning to their original starting place in order to reclaim the rights that they presumably enjoyed prior to the reign of kings in England. From his point of view, the American Revolution occurred between 1760 and 1775 when the colonists changed they way they viewed their relationship with the king. Franklin felt that the fighting that resulted from that change in their way of thinking was more properly referred to as the American Rebellion.[1]

The fighting between England and its colonies broke out on April 15, 1775, at the battles of Lexington and Concord. British troops had been sent to confiscate the guns and ammunition the colonists were storing in armories there. In a display of absolutist rejection of this early form of gun control, patriots fired "the shot heard round the world." Men on both sides died one full year before a formal declaration of war.

It seems that every international war has a formal piece of paper to mark the start and end of the war. In this case, the Declaration of Independence, approved on July 4, 1776, formally marks the beginning of the American Revolution. The piece of paper that formally marks the end of any war is a peace treaty. Rather than signing our peace treaty in New York or London, peace treaties are typically signed at a neutral location. Even though France wasn't completely neutral in this conflict, the Treaty of Paris was signed on September 3, 1783, to formalize the end of bloodshed between the England and the new country that referred to itself as the United States.

Our fledgling country needed to establish a new, formal, government. The Declaration of Independence proclaims, "That these United Colonies are, and of Right ought to be Free and Independent States." One year later, in 1777, our leaders established the Articles of Confederation which bound the thirteen sovereign and independent nation-states together in a loosely organized coalition. People thought of Virginia, Pennsylvania, and New York the same way we think about Germany, Italy, or Switzerland, today. Our Founding Fathers had established a federal government, and everyone lived happily ever after.

Almost. The only fly in the American ointment was the fact that we were obligated to repay the money we had borrowed from France and Spain in order to fight the Revolution in the first place. It is important to note that these countries didn't loan us money because Americans are inherently cute and cuddly. They loaned us money for the very selfish reason that France and Spain were also at war with England. Their generosity was based on the simple premise that "the enemy of my enemy is my friend". Now that the war was officially over, France and Spain had the audacity to expect that their loans would be repaid. Each of the thirteen colonies was responsible for a percentage of that debt, however the Continental Congress was never given the power to tax under the Articles of Confederation. The only thing the central government could do was beg and plead for money.

Each state, operating like the independent nation that it was, negotiated for more time to repay the loan. Eventually, each resorted to the trick that governments in trouble always use. They started printing money. There was New Jersey money, Maryland money, and money from Rhode Island. Each state had its own official currency, as well as money being printed by the Continental Congress. Fourteen different flavors of money, and all being generated as fast as they could print it. This caused runaway inflation, which meant that if someone gave you a dollar today, it would be worth less the longer you held it. If no one is willing to accept your money, the economy comes to a grinding halt. Independence from England may have been a good thing, but something had to be done about the economy.

In an effort to solve their problems, each state selected delegates and sent them to Philadelphia in the summer of 1787 for the purpose of amending the Articles of Confederation. The delegates were expected to edit the Articles in order to eliminate the perceived deficiencies. That is not what happened. Before we continue, let's look at some definitions:

federal: Of or pertaining to a compact or league, especially a league between nations or states.[2]

national: Of, pertaining to, or maintained by a nation as an organized whole or independent political unit.[3]

The important difference here is between plural and singular. A federal government is a compact between multiple nations, so it is plural, whereas a national government refers to one whole, or singular, government. Alexander Hamilton was in favor of a strong, centralized national government, rather than the loosely organized federal government that existed at that time. He arrived in Philadelphia a few days early, with several supporters, and a plan to change the existing government completely. The plan they proposed and nurtured through three months of acrimonious debate eventually resulted in our current Constitution.

Most people take our Constitution for granted, assuming that our Founding Fathers supported the new Constitution with unanimous approval. *Au contraire!* The committee that assembled that sweltering summer was divided into two factions that argued bitterly over almost every issue. The first group was lead by Alexander Hamilton, the only non-president to be *incorrect* portrayed on American money. His faction wanted a strong central government that closely resembled the government of England. (It is rumored that Alexander Hamilton asked George Washington if he would be the first king of the United States. If that is true, we are fortunate that George Washington declined the offer.) Hamilton clearly wanted a national government, however he knew that Americans would never support such a plan. We had just finished a bloody war of independence against the strong central government of England. There was little chance of convincing the people to support a similar plan in their own backyard. Hamilton cleverly labeled his supporters Federalists, pretending that they favored a loose coalition between the states. In Federalist Paper #9, Hamilton says:

"The definition of a *confederate republic* seems simply to be 'an assemblage of societies,' or an association of two or more states into one state. The extent, modifications, and objects of the federal authority are mere matters of discretion. So long as the separate organization of the members be not abolished; so long as it exists, by a constitutional necessity, for local purposes; though it should be in perfect subordination to the general authority of the union, it would still be, in fact and in theory, an association of states, or a confederacy. … This fully corresponds, in every rational import of the terms, with the idea of a federal government."

The other faction attending the convention vehemently opposed a strong central government. They supported the loosely organized federation they had already created. One such person was Patrick Henry, who was very vocal about his opposition to the new plan. On June 5, 1788, during the ratification convention in Virginia, he said:

"The fate of this question and America may depend on this: Have they said, we the States? Have they made a proposal of a compact between States? If they had, this would be a confederation: It is otherwise most clearly a consolidated government." "It is said eight States have adopted this plan. I declare that if twelve States and half had adopted it, I would with manly firmness, and in spite of an erring world, reject it."

Patrick Henry and the other delegates opposed to Hamilton's plan were, in fact, federalists, however Hamilton had already used that term to describe his own faction. A master of political spin that would make James Carville green with envy, Hamilton successfully labeled people like Patrick Henry anti-federalists. Talk about a public relations coup! Hamilton was able to disguise his true intentions while simultaneously giving his opponents an undeserved, negative reputation. If this is an issue that has confused you since high school civics class, now you know why. Even before the Constitution was ratified, *our politicians were already lying to us.*

After several months of bickering and an occasional fistfight or two, the new Constitution was signed on September 17, 1787. Since the Articles of

Confederation were being replaced rather than repaired, it was necessary for the people to approve the new Constitution before it would become the supreme law of the land. Each state had to organize a convention to ratify the new document. How did the federalists/nationalists manage to hoodwink the general population into supporting the new plan? Alexander Hamilton, James Madison, and John Jay wrote newspaper editorials under assumed names, such as *Cato* and *Publius*. These were the names of famous Roman politicians, and it was a common practice to do this in an effort to increase the credibility of what you were writing. If I were to try the same thing today, I might choose to submit my editorial as Thomas Jefferson or Patrick Henry. Each editorial explained one aspect of what they had written, and the justification for why they wrote it. All eighty-seven editorials have been collected into a single volume that we know as *The Federalist Papers*. Any politician who tells you that we don't know what the Founding Fathers were thinking when they wrote the Constitution is either extremely stupid, or they are deliberately lying to you. I leave it to you to decide which it is.

After two years of convention and debate within each of the states, the Constitution was finally ratified on June 21, 1789. The federalists/nationalists may have succeeded, but not unconditionally. The anti-federalists/federalists agreed to the Constitution, but only on the condition that a Bill of Rights be added. Ironically, it was Alexander Hamilton who cautioned the people that a Bill of Rights was unnecessary and undesirable. He argued that adding an incomplete list of human rights would eventually be used to suggest that anything not enumerated in the Bill of Rights was not intended to be a right in the first place. As much as I disagree with Hamilton, he hit the nail on the head with this observation. However, the anti-federalists/federalists would not be swayed, and they insisted that a Bill of Rights be added soon after ratification of the Constitution. A draft of the Bill of Rights was signed in 1789, and two years later it was ratified on December 15, 1791.

To summarize this period of history, it helps to start with the Declaration of Independence in 1776. The Constitution was *signed* 11 years later in 1787. It took two years to ratify the Constitution and draft the Bill of Rights, both of which took place in 1789. After another two years to ratify the Bill of Rights, it finally became an integral part of our founding documents in 1791.

Chapter 8

The Preamble and Fundamental Purposes

The Preamble documents the fundamental purposes for "ordaining and establishing" the Constitution. I have outlined its constituent parts to make it easier to analyze and understand. It begins: WE THE PEOPLE, the sovereign citizens who are the source of all political power. (Review Chapter Four.) When we ordained and established the Constitution, we created the government using our sovereign power to do so. The reasons we did so are listed as one through six, below:

WE THE PEOPLE of the United States
1. in order to form a more perfect union, *—Better than Articles*
2. to establish justice,
3. insure domestic tranquility, *⟩ Stable society*
4. provide for the common defense,
5. promote the general welfare, and *— Not socialist welfare*
6. to secure the blessings of liberty for ourselves and our posterity, do ordain and establish this Constitution for the United States of America.

The very first reason was "to form a more perfect union." This begs the question, "more perfect than what?" Well, more perfect than the Articles of Confederation that were intended to last "in perpetuity." The twelve years between 1777 to 1789 constitute a pretty short forever—just like many marriages. The next three reasons—establish justice; insure domestic tranquility; and provide for the common defense—work together to maintain a quiet, stable society, both at the local and national levels. The goal of promoting the general welfare is commonly misconstrued to justify the socialist welfare state that began in the early 1930s. General welfare means that something is good for the general public, like highways, bridges, and commerce. Even if you don't use an automobile on the highways, the trucks that bring your groceries from other states, do—which benefits you directly.

The final reason listed in the Preamble is unquestionably the most important: *To secure the blessings of liberty for ourselves and our posterity.* The framers of the Constitution had recently fought a bloody war against the king of England, taking back the right to own property. Now that they enjoyed the exercise of those rights, they wanted to make sure that their children, and even their great-great-grandchildren, would be able to enjoy the blessings of liberty. But how? The answer was to create a political trust.

This concept is best explained by example. Imagine a man named John who is very wealthy and has several children. Like most parents, John plans to leave his accumulated wealth to his children. Unfortunately John is a widower and is nearing the end of his life. He does not expect to live until the children mature into adulthood. If the children take possession of the money before they are old enough to manage it responsibly, the fortune will be squandered. What can John do to protect the money until his children are old enough to fend for themselves? The answer: He can exercise his unlimited right to contract. (See Hale v Henkel.) John can create a contract with his best friend George. George will take possession of the money until the children reach a certain age, and then George will release the money to the children. Naturally, because John expects to be dead by the time the children take possession of their rightful fortune, he trusts his friend George to hand over the money at the appropriate time.

For that reason, the contract is called a trust. John is the creator of the trust, and his friend George is called the trustee. The children are the beneficiaries of the trust, and they have no obligations to fulfill except reaching the age specified in the contract. The money belongs to them. George is merely assuming the responsibility of their missing parents.

Americans in 1787 faced the same dilemma. They had something even more valuable than property. They had the right to own property, and they wanted to hand that right down to their offspring even though they would not be alive to guarantee that it happened. So they created a political trust. That trust, or contract, is the Constitution. The Founding Fathers were the creators of the trust, and we are the intended beneficiaries.

The trustees in this contract are the members of Congress, and every other government agent who takes an oath of office. The reason they take the oath of office is to legally bind themselves to the contract. Government agents swear under oath that they will protect and defend the Constitution to the best of their ability. Clearly we do not intend for them to physically defend the parchment the Constitution is written on. We expect them to defend our rights and property from unlawful attack. It is more than just a good idea for them to defend our rights—they have a fiduciary responsibility to do so. If government agents swear under oath to defend our rights and they subsequently fail to do so, they are guilty of breach of contract.

One purpose of the Constitution was to create a government more powerful than the one outlined by the Articles of Confederation, but not so powerful that it could interfere in the details of your personal life. The Constitution establishes a separation of powers, dividing our government into three distinct branches to prevent any single branch from exercising too much control. This is one of the many checks and balances deliberately built into the system. The Constitution places explicit limitations on the powers of government.

Thomas Jefferson reportedly wrote, "Let no more be said about confidence in men, but rather, bind them down from mischief with the chains of the Constitution." Although some sections of the Constitution grant the government power and privileges, other sections explicitly prohibit the government from doing certain things. The Constitution is, in part, a "negative authority" exemplified by the phrase, "Congress shall make no law ..."

Before we begin to examine the Constitution itself, you should be familiar with its overall structure. The Constitution is divided into Articles, Sections, and clauses. There are seven Articles identified by Roman numerals, such as I, II, III, etc. Each Article may contain several Sections identified by the Arabic numbers you use every day. (1, 2, 3, etc.) Each Section may be further subdivided into clauses, or sentences, that are not numbered at all. The beginning of each clause is usually indented, but you are expected to count manually from the beginning of each Section. Using this outline, I can refer you to specific clauses in the Constitution. For example, Article IV, Section 4, clause 1 states (in part) "The United States shall guarantee to every State in this Union a Republican Form of Government ..." The United States is *not* a democracy. At least ... it's not supposed to be. For the sake of clarity and brevity, subsequent chapters of this book will specify the Article, Section and clause with numbers separated by periods. The clause just mentioned will be identified as 4.4.1

Now that we understand the context in which the Constitution was written, and some of the underlying assumptions about the flow of power from We the People to the government, let us finally begin to examine each of the Articles themselves. Before we can enforce the constitutional limitations on government authority, we have to familiarize ourselves with the powers and privileges they have been granted.

CHAPTER 9

Article I—The Legislative Branch

Our government is divided into three main branches: legislative, executive, and judicial. It is not a coincidence that Articles I, II, and III establish the legislative, executive, and judicial branches, respectively. Everything there is to be said about Congress is contained in Article I. Let's begin with something that is obvious to everyone.

1.1.1 All legislative Powers herein granted shall be vested in a Congress of the United States, which shall consist of a Senate and House of Representatives.

Although this statement appears self-explanatory to us today, it nearly prevented the Constitution from being written, much less, ratified by the states. We the People were planning to grant the government power, but how was that power (e.g., representation) to be divided among the states?

Large states, such as New York and Virginia, insisted that power should be based on population so that each person would be represented equally, regardless of where they happened to live.

Small states, such as New Jersey and Rhode Island, were loath to that idea because the votes from a single large state could easily outnumber the votes from several small ones. Both sides fiercely debated this issue, and the idea was eventually tabled by the committee and resolved near the end of the convention.

This argument is known as "the great compromise" and resulted in two legislative houses.[1]

1.2.3 Representatives and direct Taxes shall be apportioned among the several States which may be included within this Union, according to their respective Numbers...

1.3.1 The Senate of the United States shall be composed of two Senators from each State....

This power struggle in and of itself prompted delegates to resort to fisticuffs. It is difficult to imagine the contemporaries of George Washington and Thomas Jefferson swearing obscenities and punching each other in the nose. Nonetheless, on several occasions Benjamin Franklin was compelled to recommend that the meeting be recessed so that delegates could calm their nerves at the local taverns and pubs. The issue was made even more contentious over the subject of slavery.

1.2.3 ... according to their respective Numbers, which shall be determined by adding to the whole Number of free Persons, including those bound to Service for a Term of Years, and excluding Indians not taxed, three fifths of all other Persons.

Notice that black slaves, although not mentioned explicitly, were counted as 60 percent of a white person when calculating a state's representation in Congress. Thomas Jefferson and the other Founding Fathers are frequently criticized for being hypocritical. The Declaration of Independence declares that "all men are created equal," and yet the Constitution explicitly condones the ownership of other human beings. While this may be true, we must give credit to those men who were trying to eliminate slavery. Blacks were now considered three fifths more human than they were before the Constitution. Although slavery wasn't completely eliminated by the Constitution, it had been dealt a fatal blow.

1.9.1 The Migration or Importation of such Persons as any of the States now existing shall think proper to admit, shall not be prohibited by the Congress prior to the Year one thousand eight hundred and eight, but a Tax or duty may be imposed on such Importation, not exceeding ten dollars for each Person.

Although slavery could not be prohibited prior to 1808, it could be taxed. This clause also left the door open for its prohibition *after* 1808. Eventually the

Thirteenth Amendment did precisely that when it was ratified on December 6, 1865. How can anyone consider the study of the Constitution boring with this kind of drama taking center stage?

The Constitution says that the number of Representatives in the House will be "apportioned to their respective numbers." Did the founding father expect us to count everybody in the entire country? Absolutely.

1.2.3 The actual Enumeration shall be made within three Years after the first Meeting of the Congress of the United States, and within every subsequent Term of ten Years, in such Manner as they shall by Law direct …

We take a census of everyone in the United States every ten years, not only because it's a good idea, but because the Constitution *requires* it. Does the federal/national government have a right to ask you how many people live in your home? Yes. Does the federal/national government have a right to ask you your race, your religion, how much money you make, or where you will spend your vacation? No. Absolutely not. This is just a small example of the federal/national government overstepping its authority, but it is evidence of a dangerous trend.

1.3.1 The Senate of the United States shall be composed of two Senators from each State, chosen by the Legislature thereof, for six Years; and each Senator shall have one Vote.

Originally, our senators were chosen by the state legislatures. This was another one of the many checks and balances designed into the system because it gave the states some control over who was elected to go to Washington. The Seventeenth Amendment changed this to allow the election of Senators through a popular vote by the people.

Seventeenth Amendment: The Senate of the United States shall be composed of two Senators from each State, elected by the people thereof, for six years; and each Senator shall have one vote.

Unfortunately this is not a good idea. It further erodes the idea of states rights and moves the United States closer toward being a democracy ruled by the majority.

Furthermore, it has been suggested that the Seventeenth Amendment was never properly ratified in 1913. This seems perfectly reasonable to me, considering the circumstances at the time. More on that when we discuss the Sixteenth Amendment.

1.3.2 Immediately after [the Senate] shall be assembled in Consequence of the first Election, they shall be divided as equally as may be into three Classes … so that one third may be chosen every second Year;

Members of the Senate are elected for six-year terms, however they do not all face reelection at the same time. This ensures some stability in the Senate because it prevents a majority of Senators from beginning their first term at the same time. By staggering the elections there are always members of the Senate who have a few years of experience to draw from.

In the first chapter I explicitly accuse all three branches of government of violating the Constitution. There is one short clause in the Constitution that is often overlooked, but it may be the key to restoring constitutional limitations on government.

1.4.2 The Congress shall assemble at least once in every Year, and such Meeting shall be on the first Monday in December, unless they shall by Law appoint a different Day.

This clause is very straightforward, but why would the convention delegates waste the time and ink to record this? This clause is completely meaningless when you consider that Congress is in session nearly eleven months each year. However the framers were creating a limited government that was given very few actual powers. They were concerned that our representatives might appear in Congress after celebrating their election victories, and then return to their home states for the next twenty-three months. They did not want the ship of state to veer off course with no one at the helm. This clause only makes sense when you realize how little Congress is actually authorized to do. Article I, Section 8, is a list of eighteen clauses that grant Congress specific privileges that We the People can revoke anytime we may deem it appropriate. It is my sincere hope that this book will help you find the courage and moral outrage to at least limit Congress to the powers enumerated in this Section.

1.8.1 The Congress shall have Power To lay and collect Taxes, Duties, Imposts and Excises, to pay the Debts and provide for the common Defence (sic) and general Welfare of the United States; but all Duties, Imposts and Excises shall be uniform throughout the United States;

Notice that there are only three reasons that Congress may collect these taxes: 1) to pay the debts; 2) for common defense; and 3) the general welfare. This clause does not say that "Congress may lay and collect Taxes every April 15 for any damn thing they want," however that is a close approximation of the way Congress operates today. Congress is considering a bill that will allocate an additional $87 billion dollars to help rebuild Iraq after the recent war in that country.[2] That equates to more than $300 for every man, woman, and child in the United States.[3]

1.8.5 To coin Money, regulate the Value thereof, and of foreign Coin, and fix the Standard of Weights and Measures;

Notice that Congress has only been given the power to coin money. The original clause proposed during the 1787 convention read, "The legislature of the United States shall have power to coin money, to regulate the value of foreign coin, to borrow money and emit bills on the credit of the United States."[4] Allowing Congress to "emit bills" would have given them the power to print money that was not redeemable into gold and silver coins. Most of the delegates were vehemently opposed to such a measure. It was the uncontrolled printing of money by each of the states that had ruined the economy through hyperinflation and created the need to amend the Articles of Confederation in the first place.

Furthermore, the power to "fix the standard of weights and measures" was directly related to the value of money. One dollar was equivalent to a specified weight in silver. Similarly, one ounce of gold was the basis for a specified number of dollars. It is necessary for the government to define what constitutes an ounce in order to maintain a fixed economy. But what if the economy is not fixed? Whenever the Federal Reserve prints money out of thin air, they devalue the money that you already possess in your wallet. Imagine trying to win a football game when the referee is allowed to extend the goal line another ten yards after each down. Under these circumstances the rules of the game are certainly not fixed.

The rules of our economy under the control of the Federal Reserve are not fixed either—which explains why our economy is so badly broken.

Notice that 1.8.5 grants *Congress* the power to coin money. It does not grant Congress the power to transfer that authority to another agency. Anyone who wishes to become a police officer must successfully graduate from the appropriate academy before the city or county issues them a badge and a gun. Then and only then can they assume the responsibility of directing traffic and writing parking tickets.

Does a police officer have the authority to hand you his or her badge and gun so you can direct traffic while they eat a leisurely lunch? I don't think so.

The city or county assigns those responsibilities to the officer, and those powers are not transferable.

So it is with Congress. We assign Congress the responsibility of regulating the value of our money. That power is not transferable. I do not deny that Congress could subcontract the actual printing of paper money, or the minting of new coins, but that is not what they did. Congress presumed to transfer the authority to set the value of our money to a private company with the deliberately misleading name of Federal Reserve Bank.[5] Federal Express is not part of the U.S. Post Office, and the Federal Reserve is not part of the federal/national government. Furthermore, only a fraction of our money is held in reserve, which is why it is (accurately) called a fractional reserve system. Therefore, the Federal Reserve Act passed by Congress at 11:30 p.m. on December 23, 1913, is totally, completely, and unquestionably unconstitutional. The mere fact that this law came into existence in the middle of the night, two days before Christmas should make even the most naïve person more than a little suspicious.

1.8.6 To provide for the Punishment of counterfeiting the Securities and current Coin of the United States;

Our money system is so important that one of the eighteen privileges granted to Congress is specifically the power to punish counterfeiting. It is obvious that you are not allowed to print your own dollar bills, but think about why that is true. Money only represents the work that it takes to earn it. If I were allowed to spend money that I printed on my color laser printer, I would be cheating the system because I hadn't done the work necessary to earn the money I printed. Ironically, the Federal Reserve has been granted a monopoly allowing them to counterfeit our money—and they get very angry when someone tries to compete with their business. This concept is summarized very nicely by a bumper sticker that reads, "DON'T STEAL—THE GOVERNMENT HATES COMPETITION."

1.8.9 To constitute Tribunals inferior to the supreme Court;

Congress can create agencies that look just like the courts established by Article III, however they are only administrative tribunals that do not have the force of law. We will examine this difference more closely when we discuss the Supreme Court and Article III.

1.8.11 To declare War, grant Letters of Marque and Reprisal, and make Rules concerning Captures on Land and Water;

In order to "provide for the common defense," Congress was given the exclusive power to declare war on other nations. On one hand, this was to prevent skirmishes between Texas and Mexico, or Montana and Canada, from escalating into a war that involves all of the other states. Perhaps more importantly, it was to prevent the possibility that the president could single-handedly trigger a war that kills large numbers of people in both countries.

I repeat that only Congress has the authority to declare war on another country. The last time that happened was at the beginning of World War II. Congress does not have the power to send the president an inter-office memo saying that they will not censure him if he should choose to go to war, but that is essentially what has happened in our war with Iraq. Without getting into a debate about whether or not the United States should be there, the fact that we are there without a formal declaration of war by Congress makes our actions in that country unconstitutional. The same thing can be said for our involvement in Korea, Vietnam, Grenada, Panama, and every other police action we have been involved with during the last fifty years. It is little wonder that there are hundreds of countries, and millions of people around the world who are "less than thrilled" with the actions and foreign policy of the United States.

Our American military forces are arguably the most powerful in the world, with the ability to destroy any other nation by stomping it into the ground. If Congress has the power to completely annihilate another country by declaring war, doesn't it seem reasonable that Congress also has the power to take less drastic action? What if another country perpetrates an act that requires some form of retaliation, but certainly doesn't require us to mobilize 100,000 troops in order to stomp them into the ground? Isn't there some way to retaliate against the offending country without getting the whole country involved?

In Hollywood, whenever the world is threatened by a megalomaniac intent on destroying the world (or even a single continent), we simply enlist the aid of someone like James Bond, whom we know as the beloved 007. Bond fans know that the double zero signifies that our hero is licensed to kill. Pretty cool, huh? But is a license to kill an idea limited to the fantasies of Ian Fleming? Certainly not. The letters of Marque and Reprisal mentioned in 1.8.11 allow Congress to absolve someone of the danger of going to jail for murder whenever circumstances require the option of termination with extreme prejudice.[6]

Instead of sending thousands of troops (and billions of dollars) to Iraq in order to assassinate Saddam Hussein, I'm quite sure that one or two squads of Navy Seals or Army Rangers could accomplish the job with far less fanfare. Of course, it was Osama Bin Laden and his notorious band of Al Quaeda henchmen who are suspected of destroying the World Trade Center. The political excuses that shifted our attention from Afghanistan to Iraq would violate even the flexible plot requirements for an acceptable James Bond movie.

To continue, Congress shall have power:

1.8.12 To raise and support Armies, but no Appropriation of Money to that Use shall be for a longer Term than two Years;

1.8.13 To provide and maintain a Navy;

Congress has the power to create land and naval forces. Please notice that Congress can create a Navy without a specified time limit. However, when Congress raises an Army, "no appropriation of money to that use shall be for a longer term than two years." Early Americans did not feel it was necessary to maintain a standing Army. The Founding Fathers were gravely concerned about the threat that armed soldiers pose to a civilian population. Some of those concerns are documented in the Declaration of Independence, which contains a list of grievances against King George in an effort to justify the American Revolution. Some of those complaints were:

He has kept among us, in times of peace, Standing Armies without the Consent of our legislatures.

He has affected to render the Military independent of and superior to the Civil power.

For quartering large bodies of armed troops among us:

For protecting them, by a mock Trial, from Punishment for any Murders which they should commit on the Inhabitants of these States:

By definition, a Navy exists on the open ocean where it poses a minimal threat to civilians. In contrast, an Army of soldiers can march into a town and forcibly take food and other property belonging to the Citizens. This concern is also addressed by the Third Amendment, which reads:

Third Amendment: No Soldier shall, in time of peace be quartered in any house, without the consent of the Owner, nor in time of war, but in a manner to be prescribed by law.

The purpose of a military force is presumably "to provide a common defense," but a powerful military that gets out of control can seriously threaten the people it is supposed to protect. That is why the Founding Fathers were more comfortable with a militia comprised of the citizens. The definition of militia is:

militia: a part of the organized armed forces of a country liable to call only in an emergency[7]

Two of the eighteen powers delegated to Congress grants them control of the militia.

1.8.15 To provide for calling forth the Militia …

1.8.16 To provide for organizing, arming, and disciplining, the Militia …

The idea of citizen/soldiers probably strikes most Americans as an outdated, obsolete—perhaps even dangerous—form of national defense. However, Switzerland is world-famous not only for its chocolate, but also for its neutrality. How is it possible for a country to avoid the devastation of war for more than 200 years? Perhaps it is the fact that Switzerland has a standing army of only 6,000 troops. On the other hand, every adult male gets two years of military training where they learn how to use an automatic rifle. Because they take that rifle home with them, that country can mobilize 240,000 civilian troops in 24 hours.[8]

I have heard the same story several times about a German general who was on a diplomatic mission (read "scouting party") in Switzerland. When told by the Swiss commander that there were a million Swiss soldiers available to defend their small, mountainous country, the German general posed the question, "What would you do if 5 million (German?) soldiers crossed your borders?" The Swiss commander presumably replied, "Each soldier would shoot five times, then go home." Even if that story is only urban legend, it accurately describes the confidence a country feels knowing that every able-bodied person is available to protect its sovereignty.

As much as I may love the Constitution, I concede that it has some serious flaws in it. The last two clauses in Section 8 are probably the most flagrant.

1.8.17 To exercise exclusive Legislation in all Cases whatsoever, over such District (not exceeding ten Miles square) as may, by Cession of particular States, and the Acceptance of Congress, become the Seat of the Government of the United States …

"To exercise exclusive legislation in all cases whatsoever," is a euphemism for complete dictatorial power. Congress is allowed to do anything it wants. Fortunately that authority is limited to "such District (not exceeding ten miles square)" that is used as the seat of the federal/national government. Unfortunately, Congress can also:

1.8.17 ... exercise like Authority over all Places purchased by the Consent of the Legislature of the State in which the Same shall be, for the Erection of Forts, Magazines, Arsenals, dock-Yards, and other needful Buildings;

By using (and abusing) this clause, Congress has attempted to extend almost total control over much of our lives by creating other federal areas where they presume their authority to be unlimited.

1.8.18 To make all Laws which shall be necessary and proper for carrying into Execution the foregoing Powers, and all other Powers vested by this Constitution in the Government of the United States, or in any Department or Officer thereof.

This clause says the Congress has the power to make "all laws which shall be necessary and proper."

Sometimes Congress acts as if any law it passes must be necessary and proper. The Founding Fathers would be horrified to see the arrogant and cavalier attitude that our federal/national legislature displays when it passes a law. The recent Patriot Act is a perfect example.[9] It is apparently "necessary and proper" to ignore the Fourth Amendment's prohibition of unreasonable search and seizure by granting the government permission to perform "sneak and peek" searches of people's home, with no requirement to inform the owner that any search has taken place until ninety days after the search has occurred.[10]

Apparently there are times when it is necessary and proper to ignore the Constitution altogether. Any time Congress pretends that an edict from the United Nations takes precedence over our own Constitution, they violate their oath to defend the Constitution, and abandon their responsibility to the people of the United States. This is not only inexcusable, it was also another justification for the American Revolution. Once again, the Declaration of Independence says:

He has combined with others to subject us to a jurisdiction foreign to our constitution, and unacknowledged by our laws; giving his Assent to their Acts of pretended Legislation:

Given this short list of privileges, it's difficult to understand why Congress is constantly in session. Once they've created a Navy, they shouldn't have to do it again, and they should only create an army when we actually need one.

We rarely activate a militia, so two more privileges sit unused. Post Offices must be built, but beyond picking the locations, there shouldn't be too much to discuss. They have given away the responsibility of controlling the value of our money, so which of these eighteen clauses is Congress operating under when they are burning the midnight oil? I fear it may be the clause that grants them "exclusive legislation in all cases whatsoever."

We are not yet finished with Article I. Most parents know that after giving children a list of things they can do, it must be followed immediately by a list of thing they cannot do—lest there be a convenient misunderstanding at a later time. So it is with the Constitution. Section 8 gives Congress a list of powers they do have, followed immediately by Section 9, which places explicit prohibitions on them.

1.9.1 The Migration or Importation of such Persons as any of the States now existing shall think proper to admit, shall not be prohibited by the Congress prior to the Year one thousand eight hundred and eight ...

Much to our national shame, Congress was explicitly prohibited from making slavery illegal, at least until 1808. Even though slavery was not eliminated completely, the Constitution established the strong likelihood that it would be.

1.9.2 The Privilege of the Writ of Habeas Corpus shall not be suspended, unless when in Cases of Rebellion or Invasion the public Safety may require it.

A writ of habeas corpus prevents the government from throwing people in jail without a warrant and indictment. One of the flaws in the Constitution is that this prohibition can be suspended when "the public safety may require it" which is exactly the justification that John Ashcroft is using to promote the Patriot Act and other Homeland (in) Security measures.

1.9.3 No Bill of Attainder or ex post facto Law shall be passed.

attainder: At common law, that extinction of civil rights and capacities which took place whenever a person who had committed treason or felony received sentence of death for his crime. The effect of attainder upon such a felon was, in general terms, that all his estate, real and personal, was forfeited.[11]

ex post facto law: A law passed after the occurrence of a fact or commission of an act, which retrospectively changes the legal consequences or relations of such fact or deed.[12]

To summarize these clauses, the government is not authorized to take everything you own simply because you are suspected of something (such as terrorism). You cannot be found guilty on Friday for doing something on Monday that wasn't illegal at the time. It is nonsense to conclude that the government can violate your rights because there is a "compelling state interest" to do so. The only valid purpose for government is to protect your life, liberty, and property, and we must compel them to fulfill that responsibility.

1.9.4 No Capitation, or other direct, Tax shall be laid, unless in Proportion to the Census or Enumeration herein before directed to be taken.

The prohibition against direct taxes without apportionment is the only concept so important that it is repeated in the Constitution. The first instance of this rule is found at:

1.2.3 Representatives and direct Taxes shall be apportioned among the several States which may be included within this Union, according to their respective Numbers

These clauses are not superseded by the Sixteenth Amendment, as is usually understood. This will be explained in more detail in Chapter Twenty-One on the Sixteenth Amendment.

1.9.8 No Title of Nobility shall be granted by the United States: And no Person holding any Office of Profit or Trust under them, shall, without the Consent of the Congress, accept of any present, Emolument, Office, or Title, of any kind whatever, from any King, Prince, or foreign State.

The United States does not condone a class system, such as exists in England and many other countries. "All men are created equal" means that the law applies equally to everyone. The Constitution prohibits anyone working for the government to hold the title of king, duke, earl, squire—or esquire, as is commonly used by attorneys and lawyers. We will discuss this again in Chapter Twenty on the Thirteenth Amendment.

I hope you have a better understanding of what Congress is allowed to do, and also what they are not allowed to do. It may be a difficult idea to swallow, at first, but most of what Congress currently does is unconstitutional.

CHAPTER 10

Article II—The Executive Branch

Our government is divided into three branches of government: legislative, executive, and judicial. Article II creates and defines the executive branch, whose purpose is to enforce the laws enacted by the legislative branch. One of the most common misunderstandings about the Constitution is the method of selecting a president. Many people have never even heard of the Electoral College, and those that have don't understand how it functions.

2.1.2 Each State shall appoint, in such Manner as the Legislature thereof may direct, a Number of Electors, equal to the whole Number of Senators and Representatives to which the State may be entitled in the Congress:

Allow me to use Texas as an example. Based on a population increase discovered by the 2000 census, the number of Texans in the House of Representatives was raised to thirty-two. Since every state has two senators, the total number of people representing Texas in Congress is thirty-four. Therefore Texas is authorized to appoint thirty-four people—in addition to their members of Congress—who are *electors* in the Electoral College. There are 435 members of the House, and 100 Senators, so the Electoral College is comprised of 535 people who make the final determination of who will spend the next four years in the White House. Contrary to popular belief, *Americans do not vote for the President of the United States.*

Every political party hosts a national primary or convention to select their candidates for president and vice president. Each party also appoints potential delegates to the Electoral College at their respective state conventions. At this point in the election process, each party will have specified 535 people who may or may not vote in the Electoral College, depending on the results of the popular election in November. Since electors are chosen "in such manner as the [state] legislature thereof may direct," each state has different rules governing their selection. Many states have adopted a "winner take all" approach, which means that if a majority of Texans vote Republican in November, the thirty-four delegates selected at the Republican convention in Texas become members of the Electoral College. The thirty-four Democratic delegates become an obscure footnote in political history for that year. So do the thirty-four Libertarian delegates, and the thirty-four Green Party candidates. Most Libertarians and Greens don't even know these delegates exist because of the extremely small probability that they will ever be needed.

Some states have laws that *require* electors to vote for their party's candidate, which gives their role in the process all of the authority and dignity of a hall monitor in grade school. In other words, a candidate who wins 51 percent of the popular vote may walk away with 100 percent of a state's electoral votes. That is why a candidate may win an election by a much larger margin than might be expected from the results of the general election. This also explains why candidates will campaign heavily in one state while completely ignoring another.

Other states allow electors to cast ballots in secret elections, which means that—however unlikely it may be—an elector can vote for candidates from *another* party. Indeed, in 1972, Roger MacBride, a Republican elector from Virginia, cast his votes for Libertarian candidates John Hospers and Theodora "Tonie" Nathan. Even though the recently formed Libertarian Party was only on the ballot in two states and received fewer than 3,000 votes nationwide, MacBride's vote is historically recorded as the first electoral vote cast for a Libertarian, for a woman, and for a Jewish candidate.[1]

A few states choose electors from both parties based on the percentage of votes, which means that their electoral count more closely approximates the results of the general election. It also means that third parties have a greater chance of having delegates serve as members of the Electoral College. If every state adopted this policy, candidates would be forced to change their campaign strategies, dividing their time more equally between states than they currently do. If more Americans understood this process, I am certain that several states would be required to modify their election laws.

Now let's look at the actual votes cast by the electors.

2.1.3 The Electors shall meet in their respective States, and vote by Ballot for two Persons, of whom one at least shall not be an Inhabitant of the same State with themselves.

This clause prevents us from having a president and vice president from the same state—something that would "obviously" be viewed as an unfair advantage for that state.

While this is still true today, the electoral process has changed slightly since the Constitution was ratified in 1789. John Adams and Thomas Jefferson were close friends when they signed the Declaration of Independence, however their relationship had disintegrated into a bitter rivalry by the time George Washington stepped down as president. John Adams won the election, but he was forced to occupy the White House with his archenemy acting as vice president. How was this unfortunate situation possible?

2.1.3 *The Electors shall meet in their respective States, and vote by Ballot for TWO Persons, of whom one at least shall not be an Inhabitant of the same State with themselves. And they shall make [ONE] List of all the Persons voted for, and of the Number of Votes for each; ... The Person having the greatest Number of Votes shall be the President ...* (emphasis, mine)

Not much surprise here, however:

2.1.3 ... In every Case, after the Choice of the President, the Person having the greatest Number of Votes of the Electors shall be the Vice President ...

Notice that the vice president was originally chosen the same way we now pick the "lovely runner-up" in a beauty pageant. That is because *two* votes from each elector were collected on *one* list. Because the person earning the second-highest vote count is always an opponent, this guarantees that the president will have a vice president who disagrees with him. Imagine George

W. Bush as president with Al Gore acting as his vice president. It is doubtful that any laws would get passed—which might be considered an advantage in retrospect. However in 1804, while President Thomas Jefferson was saddled with Aaron Burr as his second-in-command, Congress passed the Twelfth Amendment, changing the electoral process ever so slightly.

Twelfth Amendment: *The Electors shall meet in their respective states, and vote by ballot for President and Vice-President, one of whom, at least, shall not be an inhabitant of the same state with themselves; they shall name in their ballots the person voted for as President, and in distinct ballots the person voted for as Vice-President, and they shall make distinct lists of all persons voted for as President, and of all persons voted for as Vice-President, and of the number of votes for each*, (emphasis, mine)

Although electors still cast two votes, their ballots are now counted on two "distinct lists," making the race for vice president a completely separate contest. While it is still *theoretically* possible for electors to vote for a vice president from a different party, this is highly unlikely given the selection process for choosing the electors.

2.1.8 Before he enter on the Execution of his Office, he shall take the following Oath or Affirmation: — "I do solemnly swear (or affirm) that I will faithfully execute the Office of President of the United States, and will to the best of my Ability, preserve, protect and defend the Constitution of the United States."

"Before he enter on the execution of his office," the president is obligated to publicly swear an oath to "preserve, protect, and defend the Constitution of the United States." This procedure is far more than just another photo opportunity. By taking the oath of office, the president accepts the contractual obligation of protecting our rights "to the best of [his or her] ability." The Constitution is a political trust, with the president being the most visible of several hundred thousand trustees. Any president or government official who violates the Constitution after taking their oath has lied under oath and cannot be trusted. Please keep this in mind as you finish reading this chapter, and as you prepare to vote in the next election.

2.2.1 The President shall be Commander in Chief of the Army and Navy of the United States, and of the Militia of the several States, when called into the actual Service of the United States; ...

At first glance, it is clear why people refer to the president as "commander in chief," however the president only holds this title "when [the military is] called into the actual service of the United States." In keeping with their desire to separate the powers of government, the president is given control of our military forces only after a war is declared, but only *Congress* can declare and initiate a war under the authority granted to them by 1.8.11.

Beginning with "the war of northern aggression," or Civil War, presidents have continued to assume more power than the Constitution allows; first on a temporary basis, and then as a regular course of business. When the southern members of Congress refused to return to Washington after Abraham Lincoln's election, the legislature was unable to establish a quorum. Without a Congress to "check and balance" his executive authority, Lincoln began to interpret the Constitution on his own. He decided that the Constitution implicitly granted him special "war powers" that he could use during emergency situations. Lincoln acted as a dictator for several weeks, presuming to nullify Constitutional protections such as the right of habeas corpus.

habeas corpus ad subjiciendum: A writ directed to the person detaining another, and commanding him to produce the body of the prisoner or person detained, the purpose of which is to test the legality of the detention or imprisonment; not whether he is guilty or innocent. [2]

1.9.2 The Privilege of the Writ of Habeas Corpus shall not be suspended, unless when in Cases of Rebellion or Invasion the public Safety may require it.

This clause, found in Article I, Section 9, is one of the powers *prohibited* to Congress! In Lincoln's twisted logic, he concluded that this clause gave him (rather than Congress) the authority to arrest people without an indictment, and to hold them in spite of public demands to justify the imprisonment. Lincoln's tyranny could have been worse. Lincoln was ordered by the Supreme Court to restore the right of habeas corpus at the conclusion of the Civil War. He responded by writing a letter of defiance that makes for very interesting reading. Of course, soon after, Lincoln was quite dead, but the whole episode offers an opportunity for a different view of John Wilkes Booth.

On March 9, 1933 Franklin Delano Roosevelt used the Great Depression as his excuse to declare a national emergency, thus giving him the presumed authority to exercise "extraordinary powers." Unlike Lincoln, however, this "national emergency" has never been terminated. Fortunately the Internet gives you the ability to confirm this unbelievable claim for yourself. Use your favorite search engine to look for Senate Report 93-549. Here is an excerpt from that document:

93d Congress
1st Session
Report No. 93-549
EMERGENCY POWERS STATUTES:

PROVISIONS OF FEDERAL LAW NOW IN EFFECT DELEGATING
TO THE EXECUTIVE EXTRAORDINARY AUTHORITY IN TIME OF NATIONAL EMERGENCY

REPORT OF THE SPECIAL COMMITTEE ON THE TERMINATION OF THE NATIONAL EMERGENCY UNITED STATES SENATE **NOVEMBER 19, 1973**

U.S. GOVERNMENT PRINTING OFFICE
WASHINGTON : 1973
24-509 O

Since March 9, 1933, the United States has been in a state of declared national emergency. In fact, there are now in effect four presidentially-proclaimed states of national emergency: In addition to the national emergency declared by President Roosevelt in 1933, there are also the national emergency proclaimed by President Truman on December 16, 1950, during the Korean conflict, and the states of national emergency declared by President Nixon on March 23, 1970, and August 15, 1971.

These proclamations give force to 470 provisions of Federal law. These hundreds of statutes delegate to the President extraordinary powers, ordinarily exercised by the Congress, which affect the lives of American citizens in a host of all-encompassing manners. This vast range of powers, taken together, confer enough authority to rule the country without reference to normal Constitutional processes. Under the powers delegated by these statutes, the President may: seize property; organize and control the means of production; seize commodities; assign military forces abroad; institute martial law; seize and control all transportation and communication; regulate the operation of private enterprise; restrict travel; and, in a plethora of particular ways, control the lives of all American citizens.

It did not take Congress until 1973 to realize that the Constitution was essentially a dead letter. If you search the Internet for "Congressman Beck" and "Congressional Record," you will find several instances of the speech he gave in 1933. Here is an excerpt from his comments:

"I think of all the damnable heresies that have ever been suggested in connection with the Constitution, the doctrine of emergency is the worst. It means that when Congress declares an emergency, there is no Constitution. This means its death. It is the very doctrine that the German Chancellor is invoking today in the dying hours of the parliamentary body of the German republic, namely, that because of an emergency, it should grant to the German chancellor absolute power to pass any law, even though the law contradicts the Constitution of the German republic.

"Chancellor Hitler is at least frank about it. We pay the Constitution lip service, but the result is the same.... the Constitution of the United States, as a restraining influence in keeping the federal government within the carefully prescribed channels of power, is moribund, if not dead. We are witnessing its death-agonies, for when this bill becomes a law, if unhappily it becomes a law, there is no longer any workable Constitution to keep the Congress within the limits of its Constitutional powers.

In Chapter One I promised I would rattle your cage, and perhaps make you mildly uncomfortable at times. This should be one of those times. I think it is reasonable to assume that your rights are under greater threat during a war or emergency than they are when America is at peace. If the purpose of the Constitution is to protect those rights, is it rational to *suspend* the Constitution in times of emergency—or are those precisely the moments when we need our Constitutional protections the most?

Before the Constitution was ordained and established, most people lived under the rule of a king. The king could make law by proclamation, simply by signing his name to a piece of paper. All of the presidents since Abraham Lincoln have been following that example, by signing executive orders that purport to enact law over American citizens. There isn't a shred of difference between the king's proclamation and this type of executive order, almost all of which are promulgated on the "extraordinary powers" assumed by the chief executive during periods of national emergency.

Americans should write to their legislators to demand an immediate end to our national emergencies and the executive orders that flow from them. Remember, We the People grant the government *privileges*, and we can revoke those privileges whenever we have the courage to do so.

CHAPTER 11

Article III—The Judicial Branch

WE THE PEOPLE of the United States,

    1. in order to form a more perfect union,

    2. to establish justice,

One of the explicit reasons for writing the Constitution was to establish justice. The legislative branch writes the laws, the executive branch enforces the laws, and the judicial branch resolves disputes when, inevitably, someone decides to break the law. Following this sequence, the framers of the Constitution wrote Article III to establish the Supreme Court and a system of justice. We are frequently told that "ignorance of the law is no excuse." Keep that in mind as you read this chapter.

3.1.1 The judicial Power of the United States shall be vested in one supreme Court, and in such inferior Courts as the Congress may from time to time ordain and establish. The Judges, both of the supreme and inferior Courts, shall hold their Offices during good Behaviour, and shall, at stated Times, receive for their Services a Compensation, which shall not be diminished during their Continuance in Office.

Notice that judges "shall hold their offices during good behavior." In other words, judges may continue in their position until: they die in office, they choose to retire, or they are removed from office through impeachment. The Founding Fathers wanted to protect the Supreme Court from the corruption associated with elected office. Since the members of the Supreme Court are elected for life, they are not required to campaign for public support. It was argued that their decisions would not be tainted because they owed political favors to those who elected them. It was also hoped that they would now be free to make judicial decisions based solely on the Constitution without any threat of losing their jobs. This is an excellent idea, but only if the people who attain these positions are honest and ethical in the first place.

Unfortunately history has shown that these judges have been coerced in other ways. FDR was able to pass several pieces of New Deal legislation previously deemed unconstitutional because he threatened to nominate as many as forty-five judges to the Supreme Court. Not wishing to become trivialized, the existing judges capitulated to Roosevelt's threat, thereby failing in their responsibility to limit the power of the executive branch. The result of their failure is that the United States is now bogged down in a socialist welfare state that is destined to destroy our once-great country unless We the People take action to change the status quo.

3.2.1 The judicial Power shall extend to all Cases, in Law and Equity, arising under this Constitution [and] to all Cases of admiralty and maritime Jurisdiction;

Before a court can proceed, it must have jurisdiction over the case. Imagine that a French judge has approached you and said, "Madame and Monsieur, I am here to collect 10,000 francs that you owe in Parisian taxes." Would you respond, "Gosh! I didn't realize that my debt was so high"? One would hope that you would have the wherewithal to say, "Go away and leave me alone. You have no jurisdiction here." "Obviously" the rules of the game change from place to place, and situation to situation, and you certainly can't win if you don't know the rules. The Supreme Court's authority "shall extend to all cases in [common] law and equity [law]" as well as "all cases of admiralty [law]." Let's compare these jurisdictions to see how they differ.

common law: As distinguished from statutory law created by the enactment of legislatures, the common law comprises the body of those principles and rules of action, relating to the government and security of persons and property, which derive their authority solely from usage and customs of immemorial antiquity.[1]

Common law is the body of principles relating to persons and property. It should be remembered that the Founding Fathers considered the law of property to be "as sacred as the law of God." Common law remained unwritten for centuries, since it was assumed to derive from "common sense." If you see someone being murdered, you don't have to grab a law book or examine the local statues before you know that a crime has been committed. The Constitution is based on common law, and it is the "supreme law of the land." The primary purpose of the Constitution is to protect your property.

There are only two strictures to common law: don't trespass on anyone else's property; and always keep your promises. These principles are the origin of our criminal and civil courts, respectively. If you back over my mailbox as you are pulling out of the driveway, common law requires that you "make me whole again." You are required to return my property to the state is was in before the accident, which in this example would require you to build me a new mailbox. If two people enter into a contract together, each of them offers property or a promise to perform some action, in exchange for property or promise of some reciprocal action by the other. The contract is broken when one of the parties in the contract fails to follow through as promised. A person's honor is historically based on this single attribute of their personality. However common law was considered very "harsh" because of its strict adherence to the philosophy of "an eye for an eye," therefore another jurisdiction was created called equity law.

equity: Justice administered according to fairness as contrasted with the strictly formulated rules of common law. It is based on a system of rules and principles which originated in England as an alternative to the harsh rules of common law and which were based on what was fair in a particular situation... A system of jurisprudence collateral to, and in some respects independent of "law";[2]

Under equity law, the judge is given the authority to make a ruling that he or she feels is more "equitable" under the circumstances. Notice that equity law is sometimes "independent" of the (common) law, suggesting that the rules can be adjusted to fit the situation. This is very bad, especially when you have lawyers twisting the words to mean different things at different times. Since equity law is presumably based on "fairness," it may be prudent to remember that there is no such thing as fair. Our court system is filled with litigants accusing each other of not playing fair.

Article III also grants the Supreme Court authority in all cases of admiralty and maritime jurisdiction. It shouldn't be too difficult to figure out the origin of this particular jurisdiction.

admiralty law: The terms "admiralty" and "maritime" law are virtually synonymous. See Maritime law [3]

maritime law: That system of law which particularly relates to maritime commerce and navigation, to business transacted at sea or relating to navigation, to ships and shipping, to seamen, to the transportation of persons or property by sea, and to marine affairs generally.[4]

Maritime law was established at a time when the only people willing to cross the ocean were those working for shipping companies hoping to bring back goods and treasures from foreign countries. They were engaged in commerce. The East India Company is just one example. People never dreamed of going out to sea for recreation because it was far too dangerous, and well beyond the financial means of ordinary people. It required a "king's ransom" to outfit a ship and pay a captain and crew to venture into the unknown. Even today the ocean belongs almost completely to the realm of commercial transportation. It is not surprising, then, that the "law of the sea" is dramatically different than "the supreme law of the land."

Have you ever heard the expression "the captain's word is law?" This is an expression of admiralty law. The captain is the undisputed monarch aboard his ship, in the same way that a king is the undisputed ruler on land. Anyone who flies on a commercial airline is traveling under admiralty jurisdiction. The pilot in command is the absolute authority aboard the airplane, and any threat to highjack the airplane is automatically a federal offense because Congress has the authority:

1.8.10 To define and punish Piracies and Felonies committed on the high Seas, and Offences against the Law of Nations;

Attempting to commandeer an airplane is literally an act of "air piracy," and those who attempt to do so will be treated with the same dignity and respect that was shown to Blackbeard and other pirates who sailed the oceans.

It is imperative for you to know which jurisdiction you are in before you step into court, especially if you expect to defend your rights by quoting from the Constitution. A failure to understand the court's jurisdiction may cause you to experience a legal nightmare similar to the one suffered by my friend and fellow patriot, Rick Stanley.

December 15 is celebrated annually as Bill of Rights day. On that day in 2001, Rick Stanley, a Libertarian candidate from Colorado, gave a passionate speech about the Bill of Rights not far from the capitol in Denver. After the speech, he and another man holstered loaded pistols in defiance of the local gun ordinance. They were immediately arrested by dozens of uniformed and undercover police officers. (Rick had advertised their plan for over a month by placing flyers on the windshields of parked police cars.)

Eventually Rick and his attorney stood before Judge Patterson in an effort to assert Rick's right to "keep and bear arms." The legal motions they had submitted frequently referred to the Constitution and the Second Amendment. Everyone was stunned when Judge Patterson began to lecture [Rick's Attorney] Mr. Grant. "I already sent you an order in this case. The order has been mailed to your offices. You are not to mention the Constitution during this proceeding. Do you understand?" Grant replied that he did not. Patterson said, "Then I'll explain it again. You are not to reference the Constitution in these proceedings. You will not address it in *voir dire*, you will not address it in your opening remarks, you will not ask any questions about the Constitution when you summon your witnesses, and you will not talk about the Constitution when you give your closing arguments. Do you understand my instructions?"[5]

Believe it or not, the Constitution did not apply in this situation because Rick was not being tried in a court of common law. Instead, Rick found himself literally defenseless in a statutory jurisdiction where the judge operates with the same autonomy that a captain does under admiralty jurisdiction.

Perhaps this simple analogy will clear up your confusion. Imagine that you have diligently studied all the rules of football. You are an expert on all of the details of the game. Now imagine that you are on a baseball diamond standing on second base. You raise your hands and shout "Touchdown!" How do you expect the referee to react? More than likely the referee will order you off of his field, announcing, much to your surprise, that he refuses to recognize your touchdown. The problem is not that you fail to understand football, but rather you fail to understand that you are trying to apply those rules in the wrong "jurisdiction." The blunt reality is that your constitutionally protected rights are not recognized in a court of statutory jurisdiction.

statutory law: That body of law created by acts of the legislature *in contrast to constitutional law* and law generated by decisions of courts and administrative bodies.[6] (emphasis, mine)

statute: A particular law enacted and established by the will of the legislative department of government.[7]

Notice that statues are "in contrast to constitutional law" because they are enacted by "the will of the legislature," whatever that happens to be at the time the law is passed. Statutes may change dramatically over the years because they reflect the capricious whims of competing lobbyists and our representatives in government, rather than a rigid set of principles. The sole purpose of the Constitution is to protect your individual rights and property. Anyone who tries to tell you that the Constitution is a "living document" which is old and outdated, is trying to convince you that you don't have individual rights, and that the government is authorized to take your property "to support the greater good."

To understand how any judge in the United States can refuse to hear constitutional arguments, we must look back at Article 1, Section 8, clause 9.

1.8.9 To constitute Tribunals inferior to the supreme Court;

Tribunals are administrative agencies created by the legislative branch, so they are called Article I courts. To the best of my knowledge, the only way you can tell the difference between an Article III court and an administrative tribunal under Article I is to examine how often they are elected. Article III judges hold their offices "during terms of good behavior" (i.e., for life) whereas magistrates under Article I assume or resume their duties every time there is a new election. Any time you find yourself standing before someone wearing a black robe, you should ALWAYS challenge their jurisdiction. Before you offer a plea of guilty or not guilty (notice that "innocent" isn't one of your options) ask the judge if it is a common law, equity law, or admiralty jurisdiction. They will undoubtedly tell you that it is a statutory jurisdiction. At that point you could dramatically pull out your copy of the Constitution and explain that *your* copy of Article III doesn't specify a statutory jurisdiction. I'm guessing that the judge will be expressing some frustration with your insubordination at this point. You can explain that you are a simple person, unlearned in the law, and you are merely attempting to assert your constitutionally protected rights, such as the one referred to in the Seventh Amendment.

Seventh Amendment: In Suits at common law, where the value in controversy shall exceed twenty dollars, the right of trial by jury shall be preserved, and no fact tried by a jury, shall be otherwise re-examined in any Court of the United States, than according to the rules of the common law.

Allow me to shatter another widely held belief. Most people believe that the Supreme Court is the final arbiter of what the Constitution says. No such authority is granted by the Constitution. Instead, the Supreme Court assumed that authority in 1803 in a famous decision known as Marbury .vs. Madison. The court of John Marshal wrote: "Certainly all those who have framed written constitutions contemplate them as forming the fundamental and paramount law of the nation, and, consequently, the theory of every such government must be, that an act of the legislature, repugnant to the constitution, is void."

Although I completely agree that an act of the legislature repugnant to the Constitution is void, none of the branches of government can assume powers not explicitly delegated to it by the people. The Tenth Amendment explicitly forbids it, stating: "The powers not delegated to the United States by the Constitution, nor prohibited by it to the States, are reserved to the States respectively, or to the people".

The federal/national government can only do what we give them explicit permission to do. Therefore, we should avoid the conclusion that something is or is not constitutional just because the Supreme Court says it is. We the People, participating as members of a jury, remain the ultimate decision-makers as to what is or is not lawful or constitutional.

The Eighteenth Amendment was ratified in 1919 prohibiting the manufacture, sale, and transportation of alcohol. It was hoped that this would reduce the number of fatalities due to alcoholism, but that number remained the same before, during, and after prohibition. Notice that even a Constitutional amendment can't prevent people from doing what they want. The black market for alcohol generated huge profits for men like Al Capone, who were willing to kill, if necessary, to circumvent the law. Many families operated hidden stills in order to make some extra money, especially during the Great Depression.

When people were brought to trial for making or selling alcohol in an effort to feed their families, juries refused to find them guilty. The government found it impossible to enforce the law, and eventually the Twenty-first

Amendment was ratified (in December of 1933) repealing the Eighteenth Amendment.

"Taking the law into your own hands" does not automatically make you a vigilante. Members of a jury are supposed to take the law into their own hands, contrary to the instructions they are given by the judge. John Jay was the very first Supreme Court justice and one of the authors of the *Federalist Papers*. During the first trial ever brought before the Supreme Court, John Jay gave the following instructions to the jury: "It is presumed, that juries are the best judges of facts; it is on the other hand, presumed that courts are the best judges of law. But still both objects are within your power of decision ... you have a right to take it upon yourselves to be the judge of both, and to determine the law as well as the fact in controversy."

Compare John Jay's instructions to the instructions typically given to juries today: "It becomes my duty as judge to instruct you concerning the law applicable to this case, and it is your duty as jurors to follow the law as I shall state it to you. You are to be governed solely by the evidence introduced in this trial, and the law as stated to you by me."

Judges and lawyers have taken control of the law because Americans are ignorant of their rights and responsibilities as citizens. A non-profit organization called the Fully Informed Jury Association (FIJA) is dedicated to educating the public about the power they have on a jury. This power is referred to as "jury nullification," and it means that a jury can decided that the law itself is unjust, or at least, not applicable in a particular instance. FIJA members are frequently harassed for attempting to circulate literature on the sidewalk in front of a courthouse. Not only is this a violation of free speech, it is an overt attempt to prevent Americans from protecting themselves from the "long arm of the law."

There is yet another jurisdiction that you should be aware of. It is the:

uniform commercial code: One of the Uniform Laws drafted by the National Conference of Commissioners on Uniform State Laws and the American Law Institute governing commercial transactions (including sales and leasing of goods, transfer of funds, commercial paper, bank deposits and collections, letters of credit, bulk transfers, warehouse receipts, bills of lading, investment securities, and secured transactions). The UCC has been adopted in whole or substantially by all states.[8]

In a common law jurisdiction it is assumed that you intend to exercise your individual rights unless you specifically waive them. For example, computer programmers often sign non-disclosure agreements before large companies are willing to hire them. By signing the agreement, programmers voluntarily limit their freedom of speech in exchange for a well-paying job. The Uniform Commercial Code makes the opposite assumption. The UCC assumes that you have waived all of your rights—unless you explicitly *reserve* them. This option is documented in chapter 1, section 207:

UCC § 1-207. Performance or Acceptance Under Reservation of Rights.: 1) A party who with explicit reservation of rights performs or promises performance or assents to performance in a manner demanded or offered by the other party does not thereby prejudice the rights reserved. Such words as "without prejudice," "under protest" or the like are sufficient.

No need to worry, however. This topsy-turvy interpretation of rights only applies to people who have volunteered to participate under the rules of the Uniform Commercial Code. In order to volunteer, a person must use Federal Reserve Notes (a.k.a. "dollars") in any of their financial transactions. In other words, as long as you don't use money, this warning doesn't apply to you. If this *does* apply to you, then you may want to write "UCC 1-207 All rights reserved" just above your autograph (i.e., "signature") on any legal document.

Have I started rattling your cage, yet? Are you beginning to feel like you've entered the *Twilight Zone* or Alice's Wonderland? Do you remember that ignorance of the law is no excuse? It should be obvious by now that your knowledge about the Constitution and the law is sorely lacking. All three branches of government were created to protect our rights, and all three systematically violate our rights—but none so egregiously as the judicial branch.

CHAPTER 12

Article IV and Citizenship

The Constitution established a national aspect to our form of government, uniting the states under one common authority, now located in Washington, D.C. *The* United States became singular. Nonetheless, we are the *United* States of America. Our name emphasizes the fact that our country is a union of states. The Declaration of Independence asserts:

That these United Colonies are, and of Right ought to be Free and Independent States;

This statement expresses the federal origins of our government. *These* United States are also plural. This should be no more confusing than the fact that we may refer to John and Mary Smith as "the Smiths," yet they remain, first and foremost, individuals—individuals who exercise the right to "secede from the union" in 50 percent of today's marriages. Article IV of the Constitution outlines the relationship between these sovereign and independent states, and between the citizens of each of the states.

4.1.1 Full Faith and Credit shall be given in each State to the public Acts, Records, and judicial Proceedings of every other State. And the Congress may by general Laws prescribe the Manner in which such Acts, Records and Proceedings shall be proved, and the Effect thereof.

This clause makes it mandatory for states to recognize the jurisdictions of all the others. A contract established in one state must be considered valid in the others. A person convicted of a crime in one state is recognized as a criminal by all of the other states. On the other hand, a vice detective from Salt Lake City cannot arrest people for gambling in Las Vegas. Each state has its own, sovereign jurisdiction, and Utah is obligated to respect Nevada's decision to allow people to wager money if they wish.

4.2.1 The Citizens of each State shall be entitled to all Privileges and Immunities of Citizens in the several States.

I hope this clause changes the way Americans think about who they are. This clause talks about "Citizens of each *State*," not about citizens of the United States. During the convention of 1787, George Washington would introduce himself as "a citizen of Virginia." Benjamin Franklin would introduce himself as "a citizen of Pennsylvania." Notice that citizens of each state shall enjoy "all the privileges and immunities" of the several states. Knowing the distinction between rights and privileges, why would the Constitution establish privileges that we are "entitled to," or granted? Keep in mind that each state is "free and independent." The relationship between the states is the same as the relationship between countries. I am a foreigner when I go to visit Mexico, and Mexican law will treat me as an outsider. I am extremely conscious that, for all intents and purposes, I have no rights in Mexico. The same thing would have been true if a citizen of Texas went to visit "the independent country" of Oklahoma. Ordinarily they would be treated as an outsider, and would be required to show some identification as they cross the border. However, because of 4.2.1, each state agrees to grant citizens of the other states all of the "privileges and immunities" that they would have if they were, in fact, a citizen of the state they are visiting. In other words, Oklahoma agrees to treat Texans as if they were Oklahomans, recognizing the rights they have when they are still in Texas. This is a continuation of the principle of giving "full faith and credit" to the laws of other states.

State citizens are the same "We the People" who created the government by ordaining and establishing the Constitution. Most people believe that the terms "state citizen" and "United States citizen" are synonymous, but they are not. As recently as 1966, the Maryland Supreme Court ruled:

Both before and after the Fourteenth Amendment to the federal Constitution, it has not been necessary for a person to be a citizen of the United States in order to be a citizen of his state.[1]

The concept of citizenship is extremely important, but grossly misunderstood by most Americans. Your status with respect to the Constitution, and your "standing" in a court of law are determined by whom you claim to be. Remember that foreigners are treated as outsiders, and that John Smith can be an individual and "Mary's husband" at the same time.

Before we continue, it is necessary to examine some legal definitions. One of the primary reasons that law appears to be so complicated is because lawyers and judges often have different definitions than the ones you and I might use in conversation. A perfect example is the legal definition for person.

person: In general usage, a human being (i.e., natural person), though by statute [the] term may include labor organizations, partnerships, associations, corporations, legal representatives, trustees, trustees in bankruptcy, or receivers. [see 29 USC 152] [The] scope and delineation of [the] term is necessary for determining those to whom [the] Fourteenth Amendment of [the] Constitution affords protection since this Amendment expressly applies to "person."

corporation A corporation is a "person" within [the] meaning of [the] Fourteenth Amendment equal protection and due process provisions of the Unites States Constitution. *Metropolitan Life Ins. Co. v. Ward, Ala., 470 U.S. 869* [2]

Are you shocked to learn that Ford Motor Company is a "person"? Are you confused to think that Microsoft is protected by the Fourteenth Amendment? The key to unraveling this confusion is to understand what a *juristic person* is. Juristic refers to anything related to the judicial system. A judge is sometimes referred to as a *jurist,* and the twelve people with the power to decide the facts and the law are called a *jury.* A *juristic person* is an artificial creation, or corporation, that can be sued in court.

Firestone Tires was taken to court accused of manufacturing defective tires that contributed to the deaths of people who drove certain types of vehicles. Firestone Tires is not a flesh and blood entity. "Obviously" Firestone Tires cannot exercise freedom of speech or freedom of religion, because it is merely a figment of imagination created by people. It is a corporation.

corporation: An *artificial person* or legal entity created by or under the authority of the laws of a state. An association of persons created by statute as a legal entity.[3] (emphasis, mine)

Keep this definition in mind as you read the Fourteenth Amendment.

Fourteenth Amendment—Section 1: All persons born or naturalized in the United States, and subject to the jurisdiction thereof, are citizens of the United States and of the State wherein they reside.

Notice that this amendment refers to all "persons," which "may include labor organizations, partnerships, associations"—and "corporations." These persons are "citizens of the United States and [citizens] of the State wherein they reside." This clause establishes *dual citizenship*, with "citizens of the United States" apparently taking precedence. Remember that the creator is always held to be more powerful than the created. Because Congress has created these juristic citizens, they are "subject to the jurisdiction" of Congress.

We the People created Congress.

Congress created U.S. citizens.

We the People have a right to keep and bear arms.

U.S. citizens must obtain a concealed carry permit.

We the People have a right to travel.

U.S. citizens must obtain a driver's license.

We the People have a right to live with whomever we wish.

U.S. citizens are expected to get a marriage license.

We the People have *rights*.

U.S. citizens are granted *privileges*.

In other words, U.S. citizens have no rights.

Do I have your attention yet? So how and when do We the People become U.S. citizens? Each of us has unknowingly become entangled in several contracts that are considered *prima facie* evidence of our U.S. citizenship, including but not limited to: a birth certificate, Social Security number, driver's license, marriage license, and voter's registration card. The last one generally has a box labeled "United States citizen" that most people eagerly check without thinking. We "voluntarily" give up our rights in exchange for government benefits, such as Social Security. Simply put, because you were never told about the forfeiture of your rights, each of these contracts is technically invalid because it was perpetrated based on fraud.

This may sound like "black is white," but that is a hint to how this charade started in the first place. The Civil War (or "war of northern aggression" or "war of southern independence") was about the right of individual states to secede from the union. The subject of slavery was only a justification for the war. When the war ended in 1865, the Reconstruction Acts were used to keep the southern states in economic submission to the northern states. Several Constitutional Amendments were also added shortly thereafter. The Thirteenth Amendment abolishing slavery was ratified December 6, 1865. The Fourteenth Amendment was ratified on June 9, 1868, and the Fifteenth Amendment allowing black *men* to vote was ratified on February 3, 1870. Women would not acquire suffrage for another fifty years, until the ratification of the Nineteenth Amendment on August 18, 1920.

Given the blatant racial prejudice at the time, lawmakers had little intention of recognizing blacks as legally or socially equal to whites. Therefore the Fourteenth Amendment gives the appearance of "equal protection under the law," while it actually establishes a second class of citizen, inferior to We the People. We the (white) People have the right to keep and bear arms. U.S. (black) citizens were required to obtain permits in order to possess guns. We the (white) People have the right to live with whomever we wish. U.S. (black) citizens who wanted to live with We the (white) People were required to obtain a marriage license.

The idea that your citizenship is questionable may still require some additional proof. (This is the legal equivalent of an adult discovering that he or she is adopted.) Pay attention to the dates of the following court decisions that acknowledge that there are, indeed, several types of citizenship.

Ex parte Knowles, 5 Cal. 300, 302 (1855): By metaphysical refinement, in examining our form of government, it might be correctly said that there is no such thing as a citizen of the United States. But constant usage arising from convenience, and perhaps necessity, and dating from the formation of the Confederacy has given substantial existence to the idea which the term conveys. A citizen of any one of the States of the Union, is held to be, and called a citizen of the United States, although technically and abstractly there is no such thing. To conceive a citizen of the United States who is not a citizen of some one of the states, is totally foreign to the idea, and inconsistent with the proper construction and common understanding of the expression as used in the Constitution, which must be deduced from its various other provisions. The object then to be obtained, by the exercise of the power of naturalization, was to make citizens of the respective states.

United States v. Anthony 24 Fed. Cas. 829 (No. 14,459), 830 (1874): The 14th Amendment *creates* and defines citizenship of the United States. It had long been contended, and had been held by many learned authorities, and had never been judicially decided to the contrary, that there was no such thing as a citizen of the United States, except by first becoming a citizen of some state. (emphasis, mine)

United States v. Cruikshank, 92 U.S. 542 (1875): We have in our political system a government of the United States and a government of each of the several states. Each one of these governments is distinct from the others, and each has citizens of its own who owe it allegiance, and whose rights, within its jurisdiction, it must protect. The same person may be at the same time a citizen of the United States and a citizen of a state, but his rights of citizenship under one of these governments will be different from those he has under the other.

This idea will very likely require additional investigation on your part before you are willing to accept it, however it is time to continue with the remainder of Article IV.

4.2.2 A Person charged in any State with Treason, Felony, or other Crime, who shall flee from Justice, and be found in another State, shall on Demand of the executive Authority of the State from which he fled, be delivered up, to be removed to the State having Jurisdiction of the Crime.

You cannot escape from a crime by running away to another state, because each state is required to allow extradition to all of the other states once all the proper paperwork has been filled out. In contrast, it *is* possible to gain asylum in certain foreign countries.

4.2.3 No Person held to Service or Labour in one State, under the Laws thereof, escaping into another, shall, in Consequence of any Law or Regulation therein, be discharged from such Service or Labour, but shall be delivered up on Claim of the Party to whom such Service or Labour may be due.

This clause tends to be embarrassing because it *required* states to return escaped slaves. Once again the validity of the law was challenged, and the "Underground Railroad" was established to help blacks escape persecution.

Although the Thirteenth Amendment *formally* abolished slavery in 1865, blacks were still required to use separate drinking fountains 100 years later. This demonstrates, once again, that printing and publishing a law does not necessarily mean that it will have an effect on the population.

4.3.1 New States may be admitted by the Congress into this Union; ...

4.3.2 The Congress shall have Power to dispose of and make all needful Rules and Regulations respecting the Territory or other Property belonging to the United States

These clauses allow the United States to expand while giving Congress control over a given territory (historically in the west) prior to its adoption as a state.

4.4.1 The United States shall guarantee to every State in this Union a Republican Form of Government

By requiring new states to guarantee a republican form of government, the Founding Fathers were attempting to prevent the inclusion of collectivist or socialist forms of government such as we have now.[4] It is impossible to protect private property while simultaneously denying that private property exists. This is a subtle but significant distinction that Americans must learn to make in order to retain the ability to pursue happiness.

CHAPTER 13

Articles V, VI and VII

The remainder of the Constitution is very short, and comparatively straightforward. Knowing that future changes would have to be made, Article V establishes the procedure for amending the Constitution. There is only one clause in this Article, so Section and clause references are meaningless. There are two basic steps required to frame an amendment: proposition and ratification. There are two methods for proposal, and two methods of ratification.

The Congress, whenever two-thirds of both Houses shall deem it necessary, shall propose Amendments to this Constitution,

or, on the Application of the Legislatures of two thirds of the several States, shall call a Convention for proposing Amendments,

"… which, in either Case, shall be valid to all Intents and Purposes, as Part of this Constitution …"

when ratified by the Legislatures of three-fourths of the several States,

or by Conventions in three fourths thereof, as the one or the other Mode of Ratification may be proposed by the Congress;

In layperson's terms, it requires a vote by two thirds (66 percent) of both houses, or a demand by two-thirds of the state legislatures just to begin a formal discussion about the *possibility* of amending the Constitution. Furthermore, ratification by a "super-majority" of three-quarters (75 percent) of the state legislatures—or if they are recalcitrant, by three-quarters of the people gathered in state conventions—is necessary to establish any changes to the "supreme law of the land." The Founding Fathers made it possible to modify the Constitution, however they deliberately made that process very difficult in order to ensure stability in our way of life.

Provided that no Amendment which may be made prior to the Year One thousand eight hundred and eight shall in any Manner affect the first and fourth Clauses in the Ninth Section of the first Article; ...

Article I, Section 9, clauses one and four are those that forbid the abolition of slavery until the year 1808. This sentence in Article V eliminated the opportunity to double-cross the southern states before the agreed-upon date. This ugly truth is one of the many skeletons in our historical closet.

Article VI has three clauses with no defined sections. However, I will continue to identify these clauses with my three-digit notation just to maintain consistency.

6.1.1 All Debts contracted and Engagements entered into, before the Adoption of this Constitution, shall be as valid against the United States under this Constitution, as under the Confederation.

The United States had borrowed heavily from France and Spain during our revolutionary battle with England. At the conclusion of the war, those countries expected their loans would be repaid. This led to the uncontrolled printing of money by the states, that caused an economic depression, that prompted the delegates to gather in Philadelphia, where they wrote the Constitution ... which supersedes the Articles of Confederation. At this point the United States had the option to "declare bankruptcy" and renege on our foreign debt.

There were two reasons the Founding Fathers chose not to do so. First, our international reputation would have been worthless, and our chances of financial survival after that would have been very small. Second (and arguably more important) was the fact that many of the Founding Fathers, such as John Hancock, had also invested heavily in the revolution. Declaring bankruptcy at this point would mean that *they* would not be able to collect on their debts. Therefore it was determined that "all [previous] debts and engagements ... would be valid."

6.1.2 This Constitution, and the Laws of the United States which shall be made in Pursuance thereof; and all Treaties made, or which shall be made, under the Authority of the United States, shall be the supreme Law of the Land; and the Judges in every State shall be bound thereby, any Thing in the Constitution or Laws of any State to the Contrary notwithstanding.

Here we see that the Constitution is "the supreme law of the land," and that "laws of any state to the contrary [are] notwithstanding." This establishes the fact that our constitutionally protected rights will supersede, or trump, state laws that presume to limit those rights. Valid state laws can "withstand the wind of Constitutional scrutiny," whereas invalid state laws are "notwithstanding." In addition to the clauses in the Constitution, "the laws of the United States which shall be made in pursuance thereof" are also considered to be part of the supreme law. "Made in the pursuance thereof" means that those laws must coincide with the republican principle of individual rights. The Patriot Act may have been passed by Congress in their haste to "do something" after the September 11 tragedy, but it was not made in pursuance of the Constitution and is therefore completely invalid. Several hundred cities and nearly a dozen states have already passed resolutions expressing this same opinion.[1]

6.1.3 The Senators and Representatives before mentioned, and the Members of the several State Legislatures, and all executive and judicial Officers, both of the United States and of the several States, shall be bound by Oath or Affirmation, to support this Constitution;

Once again, the Constitution is a political trust. We are the beneficiaries of the liberties secured by our Founding Fathers. This clause mandates that ALL members of the legislative, executive, and judicial branches, of both federal AND state governments are required to bind themselves to this contract with an solemn oath to protect and defend the Constitution. I dream of the day when government agents begin to take their oaths seriously.

Article VII consists of one simple sentence:

The Ratification of the Conventions of nine States, shall be sufficient for the Establishment of this Constitution between the States so ratifying the Same.

This short clause is perhaps the most dramatic departure from the Articles of Confederation. Any modifications to the Articles of Confederation were required to have *unanimous* approval by the states. It was difficult to get the approval of thirteen different states, so imagine how much harder it would be to convince all fifty states to adopt a given proposal. This would have unquestionably prevented the federal/national government from growing as large as it is, while each of the states would still be free to develop laws and customs specific to its own geographic area. Citizens would then be free to move from states with high taxes to those with a more libertarian approach to fundraising. This is happening today as people migrate from "Tax-achusetts" to New Hampshire. However it was Alexander Hamilton, the man who favored a strong, central government, who convinced his fellow delegates to reduce the requirements from thirteen to nine. It should be noted that all thirteen states eventually ratified the Constitution, but many did so with significant reluctance. In fact, most states based their ratification on the promise of a Bill of Rights that would be added shortly thereafter.

CHAPTER 14

Preamble to the Bill of Rights?

Most people are familiar with the Preamble to the Constitution, but I estimate that less than 1 percent are aware that the Bill of Rights has its own preamble. I think that it is one of the most revealing paragraphs in all of our founding documents—which may explain why some printed copies of the Constitution choose to omit it.

The conventions of a number of the states, having at the time of their adopting the Constitution, expressed a desire, in order to prevent misconstruction or abuse of its powers, that further declaratory and restrictive clauses should be added: And as extending the ground of public confidence in the government, will best insure the beneficent ends of its institution.

Let's break down this sentence into its component phrases.

Who? The conventions of a number of the states.

When? At the time of their adopting the Constitution.

What? They expressed a desire to prevent misconstruction or abuse of government power.

Solution? To add further declaratory and restrictive clauses.

Why? To further extend public confidence in the government

As I indicated in a Chapter Seven, the "anti-federalists" (federalists) were very nervous about the creation of a strong, central government favored by Alexander Hamilton's federalists (nationalists). Patrick Henry epitomized this concern, saying "I declare that if twelve states and half had adopted [the Constitution], I would with manly firmness, and in spite of an erring world, reject it."[1] In an effort to "prevent misconstruction"—a deliberate misinterpretation of the Constitution—"or abuse of [governmental] powers," the states demanded that "further declaratory and restrictive clauses should be added." Declaratory clauses make a statement; they do not request permission. We sent King George a *declaration* of independence. We did not send a request for his permission to separate. The Bill of Rights contains "further ... restrictive clauses" implying that there must be "original" restrictive clauses listed elsewhere. The original restrictive clauses are none other than the Constitution itself. Hence, the Constitution is intended to limit the powers of government, and the Bill of Rights is intended to make those limitations impregnable. It is clear that a law written on a piece of paper, no matter how strongly worded, is still just a piece of paper and has no real power to stop those who are determined to circumvent it. Ultimately it is We the People who must protect ourselves from government abuses.

In Chapter Two I explained that neither the Constitution nor the Bill of Rights bestow any rights upon us, however I want to drill that point home once again. We do not have "constitutional rights." Rather we have "constitutionally *protected* rights." The First Amendment does not *grant* you freedom of speech. It merely enumerates or documents this right in order to place government agents on formal notice that this right, like all the others, "shall not be abridged."

I frequently get into arguments with people when I claim that the Bill of Rights are special and cannot be repealed. Typically I am asked to point to the clause or legislative statute that creates this distinction. The closest I can come to satisfying their request it to point to the Declaration of Independence, which says: "They are endowed by their Creator with certain unalienable rights."

Beyond that, no official documentation exists to preclude the removal of any of the first ten amendments. Only logic (which tends to be in short supply for graduates of public schools) allows us to validate this axiom. This badly neglected preamble establishes that these are *declaratory* clauses. We are not *asking* for freedom of religion. We are *declaring* our freedom. We are not *asking* for permission to defend ourselves, we are *declaring* our right to keep and bear arms—as a warning to any government agent bold enough to "cross the threshold of the ruined tenement."[2] By publishing the Bill of Rights we are making a sovereign proclamation. "It's *good* to be king!"

Not to be deterred, some people continue to argue that Congress could, however unlikely, declare the Second Amendment null and void. I suppose they *could* burn the Constitution and physically shred the Bill of Rights. So what? That action has same effect on your rights that a get-out-of-jail-free card has on the police officer writing you a traffic ticket. As soon as Congress eliminates the Bill of Rights, We the People will exercise our right to "alter or abolish" Congress. *They* work for *us*. Never, ever, forget that.

When people ask me what they can do to help in the fight for liberty, my first response is to recommend that they memorize the Bill of Rights. That is to say, you should be able to recite them all, word for word, without looking at your notes. That is the first step in gaining a real understanding of them. If you don't understand your rights, how will you notice when some bureaucrat begins to violate them?

CHAPTER 15

First Amendment

First Amendment: Congress shall make no law respecting an establishment of religion, or prohibiting the free exercise thereof; or abridging the freedom of speech, or of the press; or the right of the people peaceably to assemble, and to petition the Government for a redress of grievances.

The First Amendment can be summarized as "freedom of expression." It begins with "Congress shall make no law ..." (I often wish they had placed a period there and were done with it.) The restriction is against any law "respecting an establishment of religion." In other words, Congress is not allowed to endorse any particular religion over another.

This was to prevent a situation wherein an equivalent of the Church of England becomes the official religious arm of an otherwise secular government. To allow elected officials to remain completely unbiased with respect to religion, Article VI concludes by saying: "... but no religious Test shall ever be required as a Qualification to any Office or public Trust under the United States." (6.1.3.)

On the other hand, Congress cannot "prohibit the free exercise" of religion by *an individual*. Government agencies are fictitious entities (i.e., corporations), and therefore have no inherent rights of any kind. Displaying a monument with the Ten Commandments in the judicial building in Montgomery, Alabama, is *not* a violation of the First Amendment because it does not "establish" a particular religion. Nonetheless, it is not a good idea for that government to do so unless Alabama is willing to erect monuments that display the Jewish Torah, the Islamic Koran, and artifacts and symbols of any other religion requesting equal treatment.

It is disingenuous for atheists to argue that these displays violate their freedom of religion because they claim to have none. Instead I recommend that they adopt the position that all of the space *without* religious monuments is a symbol of their non-belief. They can then claim a moral victory because of the overwhelming percentage of secular area. It is inevitable that I will offend somebody with these remarks, however I will not retract them because I am exercising *my* freedom of expression—and because of my sincere belief that most people need to lighten up and develop a sense of humor.

This country was founded upon a principle of religious tolerance, but modern Americans are increasingly (and embarrassingly) intolerant of one another on nearly every issue. There are fundamentalists of every denomination who make the early Puritans appear open-minded by comparison. Witness a bare-breasted statue being treated by an attorney general like it was an adulterous Hester Pryne.

Congress is prohibited from abridging our "freedom of speech." Beginning with the declaration that we can "alter or abolish" our government when it becomes destructive of our rights, it follows logically that we can also speak critically of our government, in spite of the current administration's assertions to the contrary. Any elected official who claims that political dissent marks a person as a suspected terrorist is either illiterate or hopelessly corrupt—either condition being grounds for immediate dismissal. It is often said that we should never talk about religion or politics in public places. Why not? It is unfortunate that expressing our opinions has been deemed socially unacceptable. If Americans were more willing to discuss religion and politics with their friends and acquaintances, I doubt that we would have the political problems that currently exist in Washington.

The Founding Fathers considered freedom of the press absolutely essential to maintaining an informed electorate. *"Freedom can only exist in the society of knowledge."*[1] Unfortunately our syndicated, national media now operates as the whimpering lapdog of the government, with presidential press conferences being just as rehearsed, predetermined, and entertaining as heavyweight wrestling. A significant percentage of the evening news is dedicated to sports and repeating the weather forecast. Analysts hinting at what our opinions should be have already digested what little news they present to us. This scant information is delivered by fashion-conscious news anchors trying to be more "folksy" than the anchors at "competing" stations, laughing and joking as if they are chatting with us around the office water cooler. Anyone who isn't getting their information from a variety of Internet sources is limiting themselves to worthless information, with the possible exception of tomorrow's precipitation chances.

The First Amendment also guarantees our right to peaceably assemble, ostensibly so people could stand around talking about religion and politics, openly expressing dissent for the current administration. This clause is often interpreted to include the right of association. We have the right to join with others that we like—and to *not* associate with those we don't, as long as our discrimination occurs on private property. When I host a party at my house, I am not required to invite neighbors that I despise, even if my decisions are motivated by racism, sexism, or homophobia. These rights do not extend to my place of business if it is "open to the public." If I own a restaurant, and I choose to exclude smoking, I have the right to do so because I am excluding the cigarettes, not the person smoking them. I can also refuse entry to teenagers with loud "boom boxes." The teenagers may enter, but their music must be turned off so they don't disturb my other customers. On the other hand, restaurants that refuse to serve minorities are (hopefully) a thing of the past. If any such places still exist we would be protecting everyone's rights by refusing to patronize them.

Finally the First Amendment guarantees our right to "petition the government for a redress of grievances." This means that we have the right to file lawsuits against the government and win—at least theoretically. Unfortunately our "justice" system is dominated by corrupt judges and lawyers, so our chances of prevailing in our efforts currently fall between "slim and none."

A current example of this is an effort by We the People Foundation demanding that the Department of inJustice (sic) and the Infernal Revenue Service (sic) answer a list of over 500 questions about the federal income tax.[2] In spite of hunger strikes by Bob Schulz and others, the IRS has steadfastly refused to respond to these queries. Regardless of whether or not you believe the tax laws are being enforced according to the letter of the law, you must agree that the IRS is *obligated* to provide us with information about what the letter of the law *is*! The government works for us, not the other way around. The mere fact that the IRS is actively stonewalling legitimate inquiries about its activities should lead to a healthy skepticism about the inevitability of death and taxes.

CHAPTER 16

Second Amendment

Second Amendment: A well regulated Militia, being necessary to the security of a free State, the right of the people to keep and bear Arms, shall not be infringed.

As far as I am concerned, the Second Amendment is the most important clause in any of the founding documents, bar none. I will be far more successful protecting my First Amendment rights with a gun than I will trying to protect my Second Amendment rights with eloquent dialogue. There is no topic more hotly debated by both sides of the issue than gun control.

Once again, this issue appears obvious to me, however those who disagree appear to be stubbornly resistant to logic. I do not deny that they are equally sincere in their interpretation of the facts, however I feel they are hopelessly myopic in this regard. I will start with the purely philosophical arguments and work my way toward the more practical.

The First Amendment protects your right to say any malevolent thing you want, even if your ideas make me nauseated enough to develop a bleeding ulcer. To the dismay of the anti-freedom movement, the Second Amendment works the same way. The Second Amendment is enumerated within the Bill of Rights. That means I have a right to keep and bear arms, and I am not obligated to obtain government permission in order to do so. You may not like the fact that I carry a gun; it may make you extremely nervous; you may toss and turn all night worrying about the fact that I carry a gun. Too damn bad. My right to carry a gun for self-defense, or just for my pursuit of happiness, is not predicated on whether or not you approve of my activity. Even if the number of children killed by guns each year were ten times the fictitious numbers touted by Sara Brady's propaganda squads, it would not justify the violation of my rights because of the heinous acts of others. Handgun Control (or whatever they're calling themselves these days) believes that if "just one child" is saved by gun control laws, then the infringements of our rights miraculously become worth it. This is specious reasoning because it sacrifices all of our rights for a utopian impossibility. Even if we could eliminate all of the guns (which is as likely as preventing teenagers from discovering sex) it would not prevent children from dying at the hands of brutal attackers.

Hopefully this debate will remain in the purely theoretical realm. If it doesn't, the people *with* guns are certain to prevail over those *without*. Which leads us to the obvious hypocrisy of the Sara Bradys of this world. Those who endorse gun control are prepared to do so *at the point of a gun.* Gun control advocates are the most hypocritical group of people I know. Diane Feinstein of California, one of the most strident gun control advocates in Congress, is known to have a concealed handgun permit. Being a senator is apparently a very dangerous job, especially when you systematically violate the rights of your constituents. Rosie O'Donnell is a famous supporter of the grossly optimistic Million Mom March. Rosie became even more famous among gun owners when it was discovered that an armed bodyguard was protecting her children. I understand a mother's desire to protect her offspring from any possible harm, however I resent the fact that Rosie is unwilling to extend this courtesy to those of us outside the world of Hollywood.

Suffice it to say that I will never consent to accepting a concealed carry permit. There are people who insist that the only valid interpretation of the Second Amendment is that of the Supreme Court. I invite those people to stand outside my front door the day the government comes to collect my guns. That is when they will discover that my interpretation of the Second Amendment is the only one they have to worry about.

The most popular misconstruction of this amendment is the suggestion that a well-regulated militia establishes a community right that is limited to the members of the National Guard. Summarizing my discussion in Chapter Three, communities do not have rights. Communities are abstract concepts incapable of having rights. Only the individuals *within* the community have rights, and those individuals continue to have rights whether they remain in the community or not. Furthermore, the Bill of Rights was ratified in 1791, over 100 years before the creation of the National Guard. In order for this argument to have any credibility, we are required to assume that the Founding Fathers were omniscient and capable of predicting the future. They "obviously" were not, otherwise they would have foreseen this debate and would have written the amendment less ambiguously.

Let's approach this problem from a more practical angle. Both sides of the issue claim to want the same thing. Frankly, I'm convinced that the anti-gun, anti-freedom crowd wants to disarm all Americans (except the police and military, of course) so we will be unable to resist the remainder of their socialist agenda.

It is impossible to substantiate such an assertion, of course. For the sake of argument, let's assume that both factions legitimately want to reduce violent crime in America. Let's simplify our measurements by limiting our count to the number of murders that occur. I think we can agree that our ultimate goal would be to reduce the number of (gun-related) murders in the United States to zero. Ideally, everyone in America should love one another, be eager to hug their neighbors and sing "Kumbaya" while holding hands from coast to coast. If we can also agree that this utopian image is too much to hope for given the human tendency to cripple and maim one another, let us set our goal to be the next best thing. Let's strive to reduce the number of murders to as close to zero as possible.

We can use the tragedy in Columbine, Colorado, as an example of the anti-gun, anti-freedom solution. No one at this Colorado school was armed— except, of course, the two misguided boys responsible for the tragedy. Due to their complete monopoly of firepower, they were able to walk around almost casually, inflicting death and terror for nearly half an hour before they ended the siege by committing suicide. Had they been more ruthless and determined, there could easily have been more than the fourteen fatalities that were gratuitously reported by the national media.

Pretend that we can go back in time to play the scenario with a different strategy. Pretend that I am the teacher, and that I and several of my fellow teachers come to school, openly carrying our pistols. This fact alone would probably have prevented the devastation from occurring at all. Nonetheless, let us assume that two boys come to school to carry out their deadly plan. Eventually they kill their first innocent victim not far from where I'm teaching. I respond by drawing my gun and confronting the two boys. Two conclusions are possible: a) they surrender; or b) they prepare to attack me, whereupon I shoot them dead. This is still an unfortunate and tragic situation, however, even in my worst-case scenario, there are only three fatalities instead of fourteen. If our goal is truly to reduce the number of homicides, my approach works much better than the actual one did.

You may be surprised to learn that my scenario is not hypothetical. Columbine isn't the only school shooting that has occurred in the United States—a fact that the media is ever eager to report. However the media evidently feels that an event is only newsworthy if unarmed people die in the confrontation. In another school attack, students who ran to their cars and returned with guns of their own were able to subdue an armed perpetrator. In yet another story, a teacher ran more than two blocks to his car that he parked outside of the "gun-free zone" around the school. He still had time to run back to the school, *and using a handgun*, put an end to what might have been a bloody disaster. When the media reported on these events, they only indicated that the perpetrator's efforts were thwarted. They egregiously failed to mention that bloodshed was prevented because of the presence of a gun.

Guns are like the brakes on a car. They are both deterrents because they both provide resistance. Brakes are a deterrent to unwanted speed because they apply resistance to the rotors. Guns are a deterrent to crime because they provide resistance to criminals. If your car is going too fast, it is not rational to remove the brakes. If violent crime is increasing, it is not rational to remove all the guns, even if you could. The answer in both cases is to apply *more* resistance! This is exactly the conclusion that is drawn from the research documented in the book titled *More Guns, Less Crime*.

Washington, D.C.; New York; Chicago; and Los Angeles are cities with a total ban on guns. Washington, D.C.; New York; Chicago; and Los Angeles also have the highest violent crime rates in the country. Vermont, on the other hand, has *no gun laws* beyond the Second Amendment. That state consistently ranks lowest in violent crime statistics. This cause-and-effect relationship is "obvious" to me, but the anti-self-defense crowd insists that additional gun laws will somehow have an effect on the criminals who are disregarding the laws that already exist.

Finally, imagine that you are a parent with small children at home. You claim to love your children enough to do *anything* to protect them. At 2 a.m. you discover someone crawling through the window, clearly intent on doing bodily harm to you and your children. Which option do you think is most likely to keep your children alive?

1. Calling the fire department so they can hose your attacker down with water.
2. Calling the police department and waiting 10 minutes or more for an officer to arrive with a gun, so he or she can spend hours completing your homicide report.
3. Taking ten seconds or less to remove your pistol from a locked container to kill the intruder where he or she stands.

There are dozens, if not hundreds of quotes attributed to our Founding Fathers commenting on the importance of guns. I will not waste time documenting them here because they will not change your mind if the preceding arguments have failed to do so. I am a very peaceful man. I love people and am known for my gregarious personality. However, if you try to confiscate my guns, I will feel compelled to give them to you, one bullet at a time.

Chapter 17

Third and Fourth Amendments

Third Amendment: No Soldier shall, in time of peace be quartered in any house, without the consent of the Owner, nor in time of war, but in a manner to be prescribed by law.

Fourth Amendment: The right of the people to be secure in their persons, houses, papers, and effects, against unreasonable searches and seizures, shall not be violated, and no Warrants shall issue, but upon probable cause, supported by Oath or affirmation, and particularly describing the place to be searched, and the persons or things to be seized.

These amendments refer to property and privacy, respectively.

The Third Amendment is perhaps the least known and the least likely to be called upon for defense. It is important because it reinforces the idea that private property takes precedence over government necessity. During the American Revolution, armies from both sides took what they needed as they marched from city to city. Soldiers were responsible for finding themselves suitable sleeping arrangements, which often meant "inviting" themselves into one of the local homes and helping themselves to whatever was available for dinner. The Third Amendment confirms that soldiers must get the "consent of the owner," acknowledging the rights inherent in property. "All the king's forces dare not cross the threshold of the ruined tenement." (See Chapter Four.) Today's military forces are so sophisticated they are unlikely to need shelter in your home, however they may still commandeer a high school gymnasium for their own, temporary, purposes.

The Fourth Amendment protects your right to privacy, which is directly related to maintaining control of your property. We have the right to be "secure in our persons, houses, papers, and effects." This is a generic list of our property. We own our bodies, our homes, and our papers. Our "effects" includes all of the other trinkets and knick-knacks we have accumulated in our "pursuit of happiness." All of these items are protected from "unreasonable searches and seizures."

Reasonable searches are permitted, and they are defined as those performed under the authority of a warrant, based on "probable cause, and supported by oath or affirmation." In other words, a judge can only issue a search warrant *if* there is enough evidence to suspect a crime *and* the government agent requesting the warrant swears an oath to accept responsibility for the search. This oath makes the government agent liable if the suspect's rights are violated during the course of the search. The suspect can then sue the agent using the First Amendment's petition for redress of grievances clause. Of course it will be difficult to win when the game is rigged against you, but that is a right you have should you decide to pursue it.

If government agents are allowed to search anywhere, anytime, without risking negative consequences for violations they may commit, there is nothing to prevent them from obtaining meaningless warrants that allow them to do whatever they want. Hypothetically, the government could eliminate the need for warrants all together, granting themselves the tyrannical power to perform "sneak and peek" searches of anyone's property simply by labeling them a terrorist, and claiming that they are not required to issue a warrant until ninety days after the search. If you read the Patriot Act, you will discover that "sneak and peek" warrantless searches are not hypothetical at all.

The Fourth Amendment also requires a search warrant to "describe the place to be searched and the persons or things to be seized." This prevents police officers and other government agents from going on "fishing trips" where they add items to the warrant after they have found what they are looking for. If you are involved in a traffic stop, the police officer will occasionally *ask* to search your car. They can only search the car with your permission, in spite of what many officers may tell you.

You can (if you're brave enough) demand that they obtain a warrant listing the items they are searching for. It may take several hours before a warrant can be obtained, but it is more of a nuisance for the officer than it is for you. If the officer tells you that he has a "blanket warrant" to search your car simply because he stopped you, this is evidence that your state's "traffic code" does not fall under any of the constitutional jurisdictions.

CHAPTER 18

Fifth, Sixth, Seventh and Eighth Amendments

These four amendments all deal with the rights of someone accused of a crime. Because it is so easy to be falsely accused of something, your rights are clearly at risk of being violated in these circumstances. That is why so much attention was paid to this aspect of our rights. Please note that these rights are only protected under common law and do not apply in statutory jurisdictions, which is the jurisdiction used in almost all courts in the United States.

Fifth Amendment: No person shall be held to answer for a capital, or otherwise infamous crime, unless on a presentment or indictment of a Grand Jury, except in cases arising in the land or naval forces, or in the Militia, when in actual service in time of War or public danger; nor shall any person be subject for the same offence to be twice put in jeopardy of life or limb; nor shall be compelled in any criminal case to be a witness against himself, nor be deprived of life, liberty, or property, without due process of law; nor shall private property be taken for public use, without just compensation.

The only thing most people know about this amendment is that they can "plead the fifth," meaning that they don't have to answer a question posed by a police officer. While that is true, it is easy to see that this Amendment expresses many things beyond keeping your mouth shut. Let's break it down into its component parts:

"No person shall be held to answer for a capital, or otherwise infamous crime, unless on a presentment or indictment of a Grand Jury, ..."

You cannot be imprisoned or "held" for murder or other felonies unless a grand jury, comprised of other state citizens, decides that there is enough evidence to justify further investigation of the case. It is true that the police can keep you in jail for up to forty-eight hours for suspicion of anything, but that is only to give them enough time to obtain an indictment from the grand jury. Grand juries are the most powerful committees in our judicial system, having the power to end an investigation before it even goes to trial.

Unfortunately Americans are usually "too busy" to defend the rights of their fellow citizens, and they avoid jury duty like the plague. I once heard a comedian say that the one thing that scares him the most is being tried by a jury of people who are too stupid to avoid jury duty. Most of the people who don't (or can't) avoid jury duty do not fully understand the power they have when they accept the responsibility. Everyone should contact the Fully Informed Jury Association as soon as possible, especially if you are anticipating jury duty.[1] You will discover that a jury has the power to decide the *law*, as well as the facts of the case, in spite of the judge's instructions to the contrary.

"... except in cases arising in the land or naval forces, or in the Militia, when in actual service in time of War or public danger; ..."

Notice that military personnel, and members of the militia who are acting as military personnel, are not presented to a grand jury as ordinary civilians are. Because of the potential abuse of power by an armed military, soldiers and sailors are adjudicated by a:

court-martial: An ad hoc military court, convened under authority of government and the Uniform Code of Military Justice, 10 U.S.C.A 801 et seq... Courts-martial are courts of law and courts of justice although they are not part of the federal judiciary established under Article III of the Constitution.[2]

"... nor shall any person be subject for the same offence to be twice put in jeopardy of life or limb; ..."

This is called the "double jeopardy" clause, and it protects a person from the bankruptcy that would inevitably result if a person could be repeatedly accused of the same crime, requiring them to spend the time and money to defend themselves in court. Please note that if I am found innocent of murdering John, it does not mean that I am immune from further murder charges. I can still be accused of murdering someone else.

"... nor shall be compelled in any criminal case to be a witness against himself, ..."

This is the clause that gave rise to the famous admonition that, "You have the right to remain silent. Anything you say, can and will, be used against you in a court of law."

Police officers are now required to "read you your rights" following a very famous court case called *Miranda .vs. Arizona* in which a Mexican criminal's confession was ruled inadmissible in court because it was ruled that he did not understand his rights at the time of the arrest. The Miranda warning is a simplified summary of the Fifth and Sixth Amendments. Once again, I recommend that you memorize the Bill of Rights so you will be equipped to protect them fully.

"... nor be deprived of life, liberty, or property, without due process of law; ..."

The Declaration of Independence talks about "life, liberty, and the pursuit of happiness" because Benjamin Franklin wanted to go beyond the idea of property to include the abstract phrase we are more familiar with. Here in the Fifth Amendment the clause reverts back to "property," which is far less ambiguous. The courts cannot deprive you of your property "without due process of law." This would prevent you from being able to defend yourself when you do get to court. You also have a right to a common law venue if you wish—however the mysterious absence of common law courts in modern society suggests that our judicial system is no longer as it once was, or should be.

Our government exercises a policy of "asset forfeiture" in their (futile) War on Drugs, which is a blatant violation of this clause and our right to maintain control of our property. The police will confiscate cars, homes, and any other property suspected of use during a drug crime, usually without an indictment. The property is generally sold to the public at a fraction of its value, and the money collected is transferred to the department making the arrest. This may be the most blatant violation of our constitutionally protected rights currently being perpetrated in the United States. To learn more about this growing epidemic, I suggest you visit Forfeiture Endangers American Rights at www. fear.org.

"... nor shall private property be taken for public use, without just compensation...."

Once again we see the importance of private property, however this clause is frequently abused by government agents at all levels, in order to take possession of private property under the guise of "eminent domain."

eminent domain: The power to take private property for public use by the state, municipalities, and private persons or corporations authorized to exercise functions of public character...

In the United States the power of eminent domain is founded in both the federal (Fifth Amendment) and state constitutions...

The right of eminent domain is the right of the state, through its regular organization, to reassert, either temporarily or permanently, its dominion over any portion of the soil of the state on account of public exigency and for the public good.[3]

Notice that *Black's Law Dictionary* talks about "the right of the state." This is a deliberate misconstruction because states (i.e., governments) do not HAVE rights. They have only privileges granted by We the People. No individual or group of individuals has the right to take your property, so it must follow that no individual or group of individuals can empower the government to act as their agent to take your property. Therefore states do *not* have a right to eminent domain. The idea would completely negate the purpose of the Constitution. Notice that they are trying to promote "the public good" which is another way to say "community rights." As you should know by now, communities do not have rights. Individuals do.

Sixth Amendment: In all criminal prosecutions, the accused shall enjoy the right to a speedy and public trial, by an impartial jury of the State and district wherein the crime shall have been committed, which district shall have been previously ascertained by law, and to be informed of the nature and cause of the accusation; to be confronted with the witnesses against him; to have compulsory process for obtaining witnesses in his favor, and to have the Assistance of Counsel for his defence.

The most important aspect of the Sixth Amendment is our guarantee of a "speedy and public" trial. It must be speedy to prevent a circumstance where someone is placed in jail for years before coming to trial, only to discover that the person was innocent of the crime. Since it is impossible to rewind the clock and give the accused person back that portion of their life that they've been denied, it is imperative that conflicts are adjudicated as quickly as possible. A trial must also be open to the public in order to avoid "star chamber hearings," where the accused is taken behind closed doors, never to return. Star chambers allow some "trusted" government official to announce that the accused was found guilty, and now (conveniently) they are dead. This is the type of "justice" that is administered in Third World countries by ruthless dictators.

Using the Patriot Act to justify their actions, officials of the American government have already taken people into custody without an indictment, denying the accused access to the assistance of counsel, or even the opportunity to make a phone call to alert family members of their predicament. This is unconscionable.

Government officials cannot assume powers not delegated to them through the Constitution by We the People. Of course we are told that these tactics are limited to individuals who are suspected of being terrorists, however it does not threaten our security to respect a terrorist's right to the assistance of counsel for his defense. If they really are terrorists, we will convict them and keep them in jail. If they are not terrorists, the Constitution will have protected their rights, precisely as it was intended to do.

"... by an impartial jury of the State and district wherein the crime shall have been committed, which district shall have been previously ascertained by law ..."

This clause is best understood by reading one of the complaints levied against the king in the Declaration of Independence.

"For transporting us beyond Seas to be tried for pretended offences: ..."

One of the tactics King George used was to take someone accused of an offense in the colonies, and transport them all the way back to England to stand trial. Because you had no friends or money in England, this naturally made it more difficult, if not impossible, to defend yourself against the charges.

At very least it placed additional emotional hardship on the accused, who was now out of touch with family and loved ones. The Sixth Amendment specifically forbids this practice by making sure that you are tried in "the State and district wherein the crime shall have been committed..."

"... and to be informed of the nature and cause of the accusation; ..."

The "nature" of a crime is whether it is criminal or civil. The "cause" of the accusation is the specific crime that the person is charged with. This information is important for knowing how to mount an appropriate defense.

"... to be confronted with the witnesses against him; to have compulsory process for obtaining witnesses in his favor, ..."

If someone wants to accuse you of a crime, they must have the courage to look you in the eye to do it. Otherwise it would be too easy for people to make anonymous accusations that would interfere in your life, with no way for you to defend yourself. This is why e-mail SPAM is so frustrating. There's not much you can do to retaliate against the person sending you the junk mail. Because there are no negative consequences for their actions, spammers will continue to make your life miserable with impunity. It will be interesting to see how the courts deal with this situation in the future.

"... and to have the Assistance of Counsel for his defence...."

Contrary to popular belief, this does NOT mean that you are required to have a bar-certified attorney represent you. It means that you are entitled to have a "counselor at law" working with you to understand the different jurisdictions, and the possible consequences of your actions in court. The overall purpose is to assist you in defending yourself.

The moment that you hire a lawyer or attorney, you become "incompetent in the eyes of the law," and they have the "power of attorney" to make all of your decisions for you, even if those decisions are not in your best interest.

Keep in mind that lawyers are "officers of the court" whose loyalty to the system is more important to them than protecting your rights. Demanding the assistance of counsel for your defense is one way to maintain your right to a common law venue, and to avoid the inevitable pitfalls of "volunteering" into a statutory jurisdiction.

Seventh Amendment: In Suits at common law, where the value in controversy shall exceed twenty dollars, the right of trial by jury shall be preserved, and no fact tried by a jury, shall be otherwise re-examined in any Court of the United States, than according to the rules of the common law.

The Seventh Amendment protects your right to a jury trial even in a civil action, however the first five words are my favorite. "In suits at common law …" Even if you don't understand what a common law jurisdiction is all about, the Seventh Amendment protects your right to have it. If you'd like to see a judge or lawyer squirm, ask them to explain common law to you, and ask them how you would gain access to that type of jurisdiction.

Eighth Amendment: Excessive bail shall not be required, nor excessive fines imposed, nor cruel and unusual punishments inflicted.

This is a very "touchy-feely" Amendment that makes us feel safer, however it is not likely to provide any serious protection of your rights simply because the word "excessive" is never defined. Since it is typically the judge who decides what is or is not "excessive," this is a purely arbitrary Amendment. People do not even agree what constitutes "cruel and unusual punishment." Some people claim that this Amendment forbids capital punishment, but that is a subjective opinion.

CHAPTER 19

Ninth and Tenth Amendments

Ninth Amendment: The enumeration in the Constitution, of certain rights, shall not be construed to deny or disparage others retained by the people.

Tenth Amendment: The powers not delegated to the United States by the Constitution, nor prohibited by it to the States, are reserved to the States respectively, or to the people.

The Ninth and Tenth Amendments eliminate any ambiguities about the purpose of Constitution—much to the dismay of those who claim that it is a "living document." The purpose of the Constitution is to protect our rights and property by severely limiting the privileges and powers delegated to the government. That is precisely what these two clauses summarize so clearly.

Many of the framers argued that a Bill of Rights was unnecessary since the government had only the powers explicitly listed, and that We the People implicitly retain all other authority. Alexander Hamilton even argued that an incomplete listing or "enumeration" of some rights could be misinterpreted to be a complete listing of rights, suggesting that rights are bestowed on us by the Bill of Rights. I disagree with Hamilton on almost every important issue, but I have to admit that he hit the nail on the head with this one.

Anticipating this problem, the Ninth Amendment confirms that the Bill of Rights is only a partial list, and that there are countless other rights enjoyed by the people that are not documented here. The Bill of Rights says nothing about the right to have children, but people clearly have the right to procreate. The Bill of Rights says nothing about the right to travel, however Americans have the right to do so—without obtaining permission from the government. If someone tells you that the Constitution does not protect some obscure right that you have, simple point them to the Ninth Amendment. Of course, you'll have to understand the difference between rights and privileges before you can use this clause for protection. You do *not* have the right to health care, free education, or any other socialist welfare entitlements.

The Tenth Amendment reinforces the idea that government agents can *only* exercise powers specifically granted to them by the Constitution. "The powers not delegated to the United States ... are reserved ..." It would be impossible for Congress to enact laws that are unnecessary and improper if everyone truly understood this amendment. Furthermore these powers are reserved to the States, which have more authority than the federal/national government does, simply because it is closer to We the People who create the government. We are led to believe that power flows from Washington, D.C., to the states, and finally to the people. This hierarchy is the complete opposite of the way things are supposed to be, and our country will continue to experience political unrest until We the People correct the situation.

CHAPTER 20

Amendment Thirteen

Thirteenth Amendment. [Proposed 1865; Ratified 1865]: Section. 1. Neither slavery nor involuntary servitude, except as a punishment for crime whereof the party shall have been duly convicted, shall exist within the United States, or any place subject to their jurisdiction. (Section. 2 omitted for brevity.)

Nearly sixty years after the constitutional provision that allowed slavery to persist until 1808, (see 1.9.1), Congress finally proposed an amendment that acknowledged the "obvious" fact that one person cannot be considered to be the property of another. Once again we see that even a constitutional amendment cannot force people to think or act in a certain way. Blatant racial inequality persisted for another 100 years, evidenced by the fact that blacks were still required to use separate drinking fountains in some areas as recently as 1965. Although acceptance of blacks has measurably improved since then, our culture still hangs on to stupid racial prejudices, even as others find it necessary to criticize Thomas Jefferson for not releasing all of his slaves.

However this chapter is not about slavery because there may have been a previous "Thirteenth Amendment" that has been lost to history. You should recall that Article I, Section 9 is a list of powers that members of Congress are prohibited from exercising. One of the things forbidden by the Constitution is the existence of a class system in America.

1.9.9 No Title of Nobility shall be granted by the United States: And no Person holding any Office of Profit or Trust under them, shall, without the Consent of the Congress, accept of any present, Emolument, Office, or Title, of any kind whatever, from any King, Prince, or foreign State.

The culture of England has always been based on a class hierarchy, where people consciously avoid social interaction with people from any class lower than theirs. A person's status within the hierarchy is identified by a "title of nobility," such as duke, knight, squire, etc. The framers of the Constitution placed an explicit prohibition against such class labels, forbidding the use of titles within the federal/national government. Lawyers and attorneys often place the title of "esquire" at the end of their name. If they are using this is a title of nobility, it is clearly in violation of the Constitution. There is some evidence that Congress passed an Amendment in the early 1800s to reinforce and clarify this prohibition. It is known at the "Titles of Nobility Amendment," and it states:

If any citizen of the United States shall accept, claim, receive or retain any title of nobility or honour, or shall, without the consent of Congress, accept and retain any present, pension, office or emolument of any kind whatever, from any emperor, king, prince or foreign power, such person shall cease to be a citizen of the United States, and shall be incapable of holding any office of trust or profit under them, or either of them.

One potential purpose of this Amendment may have been to prohibit lawyers from being elected to Congress and enacting laws that conflict with the fundamental principles of the Constitution. Anyone with a title of nobility should be excluded from government office because they "shall be incapable of holding any office of trust."

This original Thirteenth Amendment was discovered by two men doing research in very old law books. It is the custom for each state to print a copy of the Constitution and all of the existing Amendments before any summary of the state laws. The text of this Amendment was printed in numerous state volumes between 1815 and 1860. Apparently the old Thirteenth Amendment was replaced by the new Thirteenth Amendment shortly after the war between the states. There has been some debate as to whether or not this Amendment was ever properly ratified, however I don't think it matters. The titles of nobility clause in Article I, Section 9 is not in dispute, and it clearly says that "no Person holding any Office ... of trust ... shall ... accept ... any ... Title, of any kind whatever ..." I interpret that to mean that anyone with an "esquire" after their name, such as lawyers and attorneys, are forbidden from holding public office. American politics would become very interesting indeed, if Americans decided to enforce this clause of the Constitution.

CHAPTER 21

Amendment Sixteen

Article XVI. [Proposed 1909; Questionably Ratified 1913]: The Congress shall have power to lay and collect taxes on incomes, from whatever source derived, without apportionment among the several States, and without regard to any census or enumeration.

The income tax amendment has been a hotly debated issue ever since its (presumed) ratification in 1913, the same year that the IRS and the Federal Reserve Bank came into existence. It is not a coincidence that these events all happened in the same year. To understand the debate, we must review clauses from Article I.

1.2.3 Representatives and *direct Taxes* shall be apportioned among the several States which may be included within this Union, according to their respective Numbers

1.9.4 No Capitation, or other *direct, Tax* shall be laid, unless in Proportion to the Census or Enumeration herein before directed to be taken.

Let's take a look at how *Black's Law Dictionary* defines these words:

capitation tax: A poll tax (q.v.) A tax or imposition upon the person. It is an ancient kind of tribute, and answers to what the Latins called *tributum,* by which taxes on persons are distinguished from taxes on merchandise, called *vectigala*.[1]

direct tax: One that is imposed directly upon property, according to its value. It is generally spoken of as a property tax or an *ad valorem* tax. Distinguishable from an indirect tax, which is levied upon some right (sic) or privilege.[2]

I vehemently disagree with the definition of a direct tax as that being one levied upon some right. This is a non sequitur because rights are "un-a-lien-able." In other words, they cannot have "liens" or taxes attached to them. I have a right to walk back and forth across my property. I am not required to get anyone's permission in order to do so. Furthermore, the government cannot issue a tax on that activity. If it could, it would be possible for the government to make it financially disadvantageous for me to enjoy my property. This idea suggests that we work for the government instead of the other way around. We are often led astray by subtle changes in words if we do not challenge their integrity immediately. I will *never* pay a tax on something I have a right to do. I will *never* accept a concealed carry permit (tax) in order to exercise my right to keep and bear arms. The very thought of such a violation of my rights is precisely what fuels my passionate efforts to eliminate the corruption that is so rampant in our government.

A direct tax is one that cannot be avoided because it is levied directly against the person. 1.2.3 says that direct taxes "shall be apportioned among the *several states*." If Congress passes a bill that requires $10 million in taxes, Washington, D.C., should send a bill for $1 million to Sacramento, because 10 percent of the population lives in California. California also has 44 members in the House of Representatives, which is 10 percent of the 435 total members. 1.9.4 reinforces the idea that direct taxes "shall [not] be laid unless in proportion to the census or enumeration herein before directed to be taken." This is the *only* concept that is repeated in the Constitution, which indicates how important it was to the framers. They knew that "the power to tax is the power to destroy."[3] The result of this clause (if were actually enforced) is to guarantee that every person in the United States shares the same burden of financing our government. Instead, the IRS imposes a progressive tax on Americans, demanding higher percentages from the people who have more wealth. I mentioned a progressive tax earlier in this book. This is where you saw it last:

communist manifesto: 2. Heavy progressive income tax.

The federal (not national) government created by the Articles of Confederation did have the power to tax the states, which is why the newly formed united States were unable to repay their debts to France and Spain. It was precisely this economic problem which prompted the Continental Congress to convene in Philadelphia in the first place. However they were only authorized to amend the Articles, not to replace them with the Constitution. Not surprisingly, the very first *privilege* granted to Congress is:

1.8.1 The Congress shall have Power To lay and collect Taxes, Duties, Imposts and Excises, to pay the Debts and provide for the common Defence (sic) and general Welfare of the United States; but all Duties, Imposts and Excises shall be uniform throughout the United States.

This clause does NOT say, "Congress shall have the power to lay and collect taxes, duties, imposts, and excises, every April 15 for any damn thing it wants." It does require that such taxes "shall be uniform throughout the United States," which would deny the federal/national government any prejudicial influence over commerce within the states. Congress is not allowed to impose a tax in one state higher than one imposed in another state. This clause guarantees that states share the same burden of financing our government. The taxes listed here are *indirect* taxes, which are defined as:

indirect tax: A tax upon some right (sic) or privilege or corporate franchise; e.g., privilege tax; franchise tax. A tax laid upon the happening of an event as distinguished from its tangible fruits.[4]

Let's take a closer look at the wording of the Sixteenth Amendment.

"...to lay and collect taxes on incomes, from whatever source derived, ..."

Notice that "incomes" are *derived* from a "source," so even if we don't know what incomes and sources are, logically we know they must be different things. We start with a source, and something called income is derived from it. The phrase that causes most of the confusion is:

"...without apportionment among the several States, and without regard to any census or enumeration...."

To the casual reader this may lead you to believe that the "tax on income" is a direct tax that is no longer subject to apportionment. However, three years after this amendment was (presumably) ratified, the Supreme Court indicated that this was not the case.

Here is a summary of a case known as Brushaber v Union Pacific Railroad. I have included a significant portion because I feel this issue is so important. The emphasis is mine.

Brushaber v Union Pacific Railroad
January 24, 1916

The various propositions are so intermingled as to cause it to be difficult to classify them. We are of opinion, however, that the confusion is not inherent, but rather *arises from the conclusion that the Sixteenth Amendment provides for a hitherto unknown power of taxation;* that is, a power to levy an income tax which, although direct, should not be subject to the regulation of apportionment applicable to all other direct taxes. And the *far-reaching effect of this erroneous assumption* will be made clear by generalizing the many contentions advanced in argument to support it, as follows:

(a) The Amendment authorizes only a particular character of direct tax without apportionment, and therefore if a tax is levied under its assumed authority which does not partake of the characteristics exacted by the Amendment, it is outside of the Amendment and *is void as a direct tax in the general constitutional sense because [it is] not apportioned.*

(b) As the Amendment authorizes a tax only upon incomes "from whatever source derived," the exclusion from taxation of some income of designated persons and classes is not authorized, and hence the constitutionality of the law must be tested by the general provisions of the Constitution as to taxation, *and thus again the tax is void for want of apportionment.*

(c) As the right to tax "incomes from whatever source derived" for which the Amendment provides must be considered as exacting intrinsic uniformity, therefore no tax comes under the authority of the Amendment not conforming to such standard, and hence all the provisions of the assailed statute must once more be tested solely under the general and pre-existing provisions of the Constitution, *causing the statute again to be void in the absence of apportionment.*

We now know that the Sixteenth Amendment does not grant Congress any power that it didn't already have prior to 1913. The conclusion of the Supreme Court was that the Sixteenth Amendment only establishes that the income tax was an *indirect* excise, which did not require apportionment in the first place. The only purpose of the Sixteenth Amendment is to confuse the public. If I said, "it is against the law to walk on the ceiling with spiked golf shoes," my wording suggests that it may be permissible to walk on the ceiling with some *other* type of shoe. Anyone who understands the law of gravity will realize that the "limitation" is meaningless. Similarly, the Sixteenth Amendment's insistence that the income tax does not require apportionment is merely a smoke screen.

Alert readers may be wondering why I keep saying that the Sixteenth Amendment was *presumably* ratified. That is because I am convinced it never was. Bill Benson began a research project in 1984 to investigate the ratification process for this amendment. He visited the capital of every state that participated in the ratification process and made certified copies of the legislative results in every state. He discovered that several states had *not* voted in favor of the amendment as reported by then Secretary of State Philander Knox. Mr. Benson subsequently published a two-volume book, *The Law That Never Was*,[5] which he then distributed to every member of Congress. I find it interesting to note that Congress has never attempted to correct or clarify this "obvious" misconstruction. Even so, it is not recommended that you use this as an argument to avoid paying your taxes because our "judicial" system is very biased against those who try to expose the truth. Facts have little or nothing to do our court system these days.

Suppose I gave my male readers a book that says:

IF YOU ARE PREGNANT:
1. Drink plenty of water
2. Get lots of sleep
3. Visit your gynecologist every other week

Does anyone expect these men to visit a gynecologist? It may be perfectly good medical advice (or just plain common sense) but it applies only to the subset of our population who *can* get, and currently *are*, pregnant. The advice does not apply to those of us who are biologically incapable of becoming pregnant.

Using a wee bit of poetic license, I can summarize Title 26 of the United States Code to read:

IF YOU ARE LIABLE:

1. Fill out a 1040 form
2. Mail half of everything you own to the nearest IRS office

What should your first question be? I would certainly want to know, "Am I a person who is liable for this tax?" That is a question that a growing number of Americans have been trying to ask. Unfortunately, The Department of (in)Justice (DOJ) and the IRS have steadfastly *refused* to answer these questions, and they continue to place Americans in jail without even addressing this fundamental issue in court.

I do not know if Americans are liable to pay income taxes; however, I do know that We the People created the government, and that the IRS works for us. Therefore, the DOJ and IRS are *obligated* to answer our questions, especially when those questions are submitted as part of a Freedom of Information Act (FOIA) request. To my knowledge, no one has been successful in getting an answer from these government agencies. If you are curious and motivated enough to demand an answer from your "public servants," I recommend that you send the following questions to the address listed below.[6]

Questions Regarding Determining Taxable Income

1. Should I use the rules found in 26 USC § 861(b) and 26 CFR § 1.861-8 (in addition to any other pertinent sections) to determine my taxable domestic income?

2. If some people should *not* use those sections to determine their taxable domestic income, please show where the law says who should or should not use those sections for that.

Reason for first two questions: The regulations at 26 CFR § 1.861-8 begin by stating that Sections 861(b) and 863(a) state in general terms *"how to determine taxable income of a taxpayer from sources within the United States"* after gross income from the U.S. has been determined. Section 1.861-1(a)(1) confirms that "taxable income from sources within the United States" is to be determined in accordance with the rules of 26 USC § 861(b) and 26 CFR § 1.861-8 (see also 26 CFR §§ 1.862-1(b), 1.863-1(c)). Cross-references under 26 USCS § 61, as well as entries in the USC Index under the heading "Income Tax," also refer to Section 861 regarding income ("gross" and "taxable") from "sources within U.S."

3. If a U.S. citizen receives all his income from working within the 50 states, do 26 USC § 861(b) and 26 CFR § 1.861-8 show his income to be taxable?

Reason for question: Section 217 of the Revenue Act of 1921, predecessor of 26 USC § 861 and following, stated that income from the U.S. was taxable for foreigners, and for U.S. corporations and citizens deriving most of their income from federal *possessions*, but did *not* say the same about the domestic income of other Americans. The regulations under the 1939 Code (e.g., §§ 29.119-1, 29.119-2, 29.119-9, 29.119-10 [1945]) showed the same thing. The current regulations at 1.861-8 still show income to be taxable only when derived from certain "specific sources and activities," which still relate only to certain types of international trade (see 26 CFR §§ 1.861-8(a)(1), 1.861-8(a)(4), 1.861-8(f)(1)).

4. Should one use 26 CFR § 1.861-8T(d)(2) to determine whether his "items" of income (e.g., compensation, interest, rents, dividends, etc.) are excluded for federal income tax purposes?

Reason for question: The regulations (26 CFR § 1.861-8(a)(3)) state that a "class of gross income" consists of the "items" of income listed in 26 USC § 61 (e.g., compensation, interest, rents, dividends, etc.). The regulations (26 CFR §§ 1.861-8(b)(1)) then direct the reader to "paragraph (d)(2)" of the section, which provides that such "classes of gross income" may include some income which is *excluded* for federal income tax purposes.

5. What is the purpose of the list of non-exempt types of income found in 26 CFR § 1.861-8T(d)(2)(iii), and why is the income of the average American *not* on that list?

Reason for question: After defining "exempt income" to mean income which is excluded for federal income tax purposes (26 CFR § 1.861-8T(d)(2)(ii)), the regulations list types of income which are *not* exempt (i.e., which *are* subject to tax), including the domestic income of *foreigners*, certain *foreign* income of Americans, income of certain possessions corporations, and income of international and foreign sales corporations; but the list does *not* include the domestic income of the average American (26 CFR § 1.861-8T(d)(2)(iii))

6. What types of income (if any) are not exempted from taxation by any statute, but are nonetheless "excluded by law" (i.e., not subject to the income tax) because they are, under the Constitution, not taxable by the federal government?

Reason for question: Older income tax regulations defining "gross income" and "net income" said that neither income exempted by statute "*or* fundamental law" were subject to the tax (§ 39.21-1 [1956]), and said that in addition to the types of income exempted by *statute*, other types of income were excluded because they were, "under the Constitution, not taxable by the Federal Government" (§ 39.22(b)-1 [1956]). This is also reflected in the current 26 CFR § 1.312-6.

Please send your questions to:

Secretary of the Treasury

1500 Pennsylvania Avenue, NW

Washington, DC 20220

Knowing how flagrantly our government has lied to us in the past in order to take our property and violate our rights, I think that it is very probable that the IRS has been taking our money for nearly a century without the constitutional authority to do so. More and more people are becoming aware of this simple but disturbing fact, and I predict that the IRS as we know it will soon be abolished by We the People. When that happens, death will remain the only thing that is certain in our lives.

CHAPTER 22

Amendments Eighteen and Twenty-One

Article. XVIII. [Proposed 1917; Ratified 1919; Repealed 1933]: Section. 1. After one year from the ratification of this article the manufacture, sale, or transportation of intoxicating liquors within, the importation thereof into, or the exportation thereof from the United States and all territory subject to the jurisdiction thereof for beverage purposes is hereby prohibited. (Sections 2 and 3 omitted for brevity)

Article. [XXI.] [Proposed 1933; Ratified 1933]: Section. 1. The eighteenth article of amendment to the Constitution of the United States is hereby repealed. Section. 2. The transportation or importation into any State, Territory, or possession of the United States for delivery or use therein of intoxicating liquors, in violation of the laws thereof, is hereby prohibited. (Section 3 omitted for brevity.)

The Eighteenth and Twenty-First Amendments are unique because the latter repeals the former. No other Amendment has yet to be removed in this manner. At issue was the consumption of alcohol, something I suspect humans have done since the moment it was discovered. The process of fermenting sugars is so common, that even animals can become tipsy from eating over-ripe fruit. What amazes me most is the audacity of the federal/national government assuming the authority to regulate such activity. Imagine the outrage of sports fans everywhere if they needed a permit to buy a six-pack before the big game. One of the necessary and fundamental assumptions about individual rights is the axiom that everyone owns his or her own body. To suggest that someone else owns your body, or has control over what you introduce into your body, is to consent to being a slave.

I have the right to do whatever I wish with my property. If I own a pile of wood, I can set fire to it even if it is currently nailed together in the shape of a barn. Cigarettes may not be healthy for me in the long run, but I have the freedom to smoke them anyway. Drinking alcohol may or may not have negative side effects, but even if it does, the government has no authority to prohibit you from consuming it, even if it is "in your own best interest." Since when do we let the government decide what is or isn't good for us? What the hell does Congress know about nutrition, anyway? (For that matter, what does Congress know about the Constitution?) If the government can use force whenever something is "in our best interest" then government should force everyone to wake up at 6 a.m. every morning for calisthenics in the front yard. Fast food establishments should be torn down and replaced with bars that serve carrot juice and alfalfa sprouts, since—"it's in your best interest." This paternalistic attitude that "the government knows best" and that you are merely a helpless child is insulting and reprehensible. Hitler used the same attitude to persuade the Germans to subjugate themselves to the "Fatherland."

The one thing that conservatives and liberals have in common is the stupid notion that "there oughta be a law" to force people to behave the way someone else thinks they should. These laws are based on two insane assumptions. The first is that "it's for our own good," and that they know what that is better for us than we do. The second assumption is that we are going to pay any attention to the laws that they write, especially when those laws are so incredibly stupid. Imagine passing a law that prohibits Americans from having sex until they are twenty-five years old. (Don't laugh! I'm sure there are puritanical groups who would eagerly propose such legislation if they thought they could get away with it.) I was addressing a group of college students recently, and I asked them if they would comply with such a law. A young woman in the front row gasped and hid her blushing face in her hands. Capitalizing on her embarrassment I said, "That answers *that* question!" Some legislators think they can even pass a law to modify the laws of physics. In 1897 the Indiana state legislature considered passing a law that would round the mathematical constant Pi down to 3.0![1]

Amending the Constitution is far more dramatic and time-consuming that just "passing a law." It requires a supra-majority of the state legislatures to ratify it. But even a modification to "the supreme law of the land" did nothing to prevent people from drinking alcohol. All it did was to change the way people went about acquiring it. Consumption of alcohol before, during, and after Prohibition remained the same. The only thing that changed was the cost of alcohol, and a black market grew up to provide liquor because it was now extremely profitable to do so. Al Capone and his contemporaries defended their territories with force against a determined but vastly outnumbered Elliot Ness. Almost everyone has seen images in black-and-white movies where early model cars squeal around the corner, while several thugs wreak havoc with Thompson submachine guns as they drive by.

Bootleggers were the "drug lords" of the 1920s. At their root, they were simply businessmen who were providing a product to their very willing consumers. The fact that the transaction had been deemed illegal and unconstitutional didn't even slow the process appreciably. It is said that failure to understand history dooms us to repeat it, and the war on drugs is like a cultural *Groundhog Day*. Congress, in its "infinite wisdom"[2] has once again decided that some substances are "not in our best interest." For several decades now, the philosophical descendents of Elliot Ness have used force and modern technology in a futile attempt to prevent people from doing something that they will always find a way to do. When criminals can sustain a thriving drug business inside of our prisons, where armed guards and cameras watch the inmates twenty-four hours a day, the average police officer doesn't have a hope in hell of diminishing the amount of drugs being sold on our street corners and school playgrounds. No matter how fast you pump water out of the Pacific Ocean, you will never be able to drive your car to Hawaii.

This fact is so painfully obvious to anyone with a brain that there must be another, ulterior motivation for the continued war on drugs. Drugs are the only commodities more profitable than theater popcorn. People sell drugs because they can become unimaginably wealthy in a very short time. The people who are getting rich *want* drugs to be illegal. That is the only thing that creates a black market for their product. Isn't it just possible that the people who make the drugs illegal are same people who are making money off the sale of these drugs? Bill Clinton is alleged to have been involved with drug trafficking in Mena, Arkansas, while he was the governor of that state, and there is evidence to suggest that the CIA is the largest importer of drugs into this country.[3] If that is true, then the war on drugs is not intended to eliminate the *use* of drugs, its only purpose is to eliminate competition on the *sale* of drugs.

Given that the war on drugs is unlikely to prevent our children from gaining access to these substances, what type of drug policy accomplish that goal? As a volunteer fireman many years ago, I learned that there are many ways to fight a fire. If house is on fire, the simplest process is to subject the blaze to a deluge of water until the temperature drops and the fire goes out. This same procedure does not work with gas or oil fires, however. Spraying water onto a petroleum fire tends to make the problem worse instead of better. However, if you can turn a valve to shut off the supply of fuel to the fire, the fire goes out quickly, and the person who turned the valve is a hero. Keep this logic in mind as I offer an alternative to the failing war on drugs.

Children take drugs because people sell them.

People sell drugs because they are extremely profitable.

Drugs are extremely profitable because they are illegal.

If drugs were decriminalized, the price would plummet.

Drugs sales would disappear because there was no profit.

Children would no longer have anyone selling them drugs.

Therefore we *have* to legalize drugs, and we should "do it for the children."

CHAPTER 23

Other Amendments

There are a few other amendments that I would like to cover, but only briefly, to give you some idea what changes Congress has thought necessary. Sometimes it is helpful to know when amendments were ratified. For example:

Article. XIII. [Proposed 1865; Ratified 12/06/1865]: Section. 1. Neither slavery nor involuntary servitude, except as a punishment for crime whereof the party shall have been duly convicted, shall exist within the United States, or any place subject to their jurisdiction. (Section 2 omitted for brevity.)

Article. XIV. [Proposed 1866; Ratified 07/09/1868]: Section. 1. All persons born or naturalized in the United States, and subject to the jurisdiction thereof, are citizens of the United States and of the State wherein they reside. No State shall make or enforce any law which shall abridge the privileges or immunities of citizens of the United States; nor shall any State deprive any person of life, liberty, or property, without due process of law; nor deny to any person within its jurisdiction the equal protection of the laws. (Sections 2 through 5 omitted for brevity.)

Article. XV. [Proposed 1869; Ratified 02/031870]: Section. 1. The right of citizens of the United States to vote shall not be denied or abridged by the United States or by any State on account of race, color, or previous condition of servitude. (Section 2 omitted for brevity.)

These Amendments were all added shortly after the War Between the States, and are related to granting privileges to blacks—which of course is different than respecting their rights.

For other amendments, it is more important to examine the implications of what was changed. The Seventeenth Amendment is an excellent example.

Article. XVII. [Proposed 1912; Ratified 1913]: The Senate of the United States shall be composed of two Senators from each State, *elected by the people thereof*, for six years; and each Senator shall have one vote.

Compare this to the original clause in Article I.

1.3.1 The Senate of the United States shall be composed of two Senators from each State, *chosen by the Legislature thereof*, for six Years; and each Senator shall have one Vote.

Among the many "checks and balances" deliberately introduced into the Constitution was the privilege of the state legislatures to pick the members of the Senate. We the People controlled the House, and the states controlled the Senate. This established a check on the powers of the federal/national government, balancing authority towards states rights. State legislators could jealously guard their authority by electing senators who would prevent a gradual shift toward a more centralized government. This was also seen as a way to provide more stability to the government, since the people were thought to be more fickle, basing their decisions on the heated emotions of the moment.

When the Seventeenth Amendment was ratified, it was like untying a boat from the dock on a calm day. The boat slowly but surely drifts away from where it was intended to be. Without any interference by the states, the federal/national government has been allowed to assume a vast array of powers previously retained by the states. Nearly every federal/national grant requires the state government to comply with certain requirements. If states want federal/national money for building new roads and bridges (and all of them do), they must agree to enforce speed limits and seat belt laws—giving Washington, D.C., control over aspects of our lives that were never envisioned by our founders.

The Eighteenth Amendment establishing prohibition was ratified on January 16, 1919, having been thrust upon us "in our own best interest" by the axe-wielding Carrie Nation and a rapidly growing women's movement. It should be no surprise, therefore, that one year later women claimed their right to vote with the ratification of the Nineteenth Amendment.

Article. [XIX.] [Proposed 1919; Ratified 08/18/1920]: The right of citizens of the United States to vote shall not be denied or abridged by the United States or by any State on account of sex.

People tend to take their freedoms for granted, however it always causes me to speculate on the implied value of women relative to slaves when I observe that black men were allowed to vote fifty years earlier than women. Of course, the Fifteenth Amendment only made it *legal* for blacks to vote. It was necessary to pass the Twenty-Fourth Amendment as recently as 1964 in order to eliminate the "Jim Crow" laws that made it difficult, if not impossible, for blacks to *exercise* the rights they presumably had for ninety-four years.

Article. [XXIV.] [Proposed 1962; Ratified 01/23/1964]: Section. 1. The right of citizens of the United States to vote in any primary or other election for president or vice President, for electors for President or Vice President, or for Senator or Representative in Congress, shall not be denied or abridged by the United States or any State by reason of failure to pay any poll tax or other tax.

George Washington adamantly declined a third term in office, and every president since then has respected that unwritten rule. Every president except Franklin Delano Roosevelt. In spite of FDR's popularity while in office, Congress decided to protect themselves from another "king elected by the people," so they ratified the Twenty-Second Amendment.

Article. [XXII.] [Proposed 1947; Ratified 1951]: Section. 1. No person shall be elected to the office of the President more than twice, ...

In 1967, while Lyndon Baines Johnson was in the Oval Office, an amendment was passed that established a procedure for the president to temporarily remove himself from office.

Article. [XXV.] [Proposed 1965; Ratified 1967]: Section. 3. Whenever the President transmits to the President pro tempore of the Senate and the Speaker of the House of Representatives his written declaration that he is unable to discharge the powers and duties of his office, and until he transmits to them a written declaration to the contrary, such powers and duties shall be discharged by the Vice President as Acting President.

Section 4 of this Amendment establishes a similar procedure for the vice president and Congress to temporarily remove the president from office.

Finally, to amazement of many, the "supreme law of the land" was last amended in 1992.

Article. [XXVII.] [Proposed 1789; Ratified 1992]: No law, varying the compensation for the services of the Senators and Representatives, shall take effect, until an election of Representatives shall have intervened.

Can you remember what you were doing on the day we changed the Constitution? Did you participate in debates around the water cooler discussing the pros and cons of this amendment? Probably not. What is interesting about this amendment is that it was proposed in 1789. The original Bill of Rights had *twelve* proposed amendments, where the famous "well regulated militia" was listed as "Article Fourth." The first two Amendments were never ratified, because they had nothing to do with individual rights, however various states voted to ratify "number two" over the course of many years. Eventually enough states had done so that it met the required three-fourths rule, and was adopted.

Although it is obvious that the Constitution can be amended, I would like to dispel the popular idea that it is a "living document" that has to be loosely interpreted as times change. This idea is a devious and dangerous excuse being used to eliminate the few remaining limitations that the federal/national government still respects. Keep in mind that the only purpose of the Constitution is to protect your individual rights by establishing strict limitations on government. The principles of the Constitution remain valid as long as we are human.

I do not want Congress "loosely interpreting" my rights, or granting themselves permission to ignore the limitations on their power whenever they find them inconvenient. The Constitution is supposed to make it inconvenient for them to exceed their authority!

Thomas Jefferson said, "Let us bind down the government with the *chains* of the Constitution." He did not suggest that we bind down government with the "bungee cord" of the Constitution. We want the Constitution to be rigidly interpreted. As a sixteen-year-old girl once pointed out to me, the rules in *Animal Farm* began as, "All animals are created equal," however they were later amended to include, "but some animals are more equal than others." I leave you with the words of Patrick Henry who, in 1788, said: "Guard with jealous attention the public liberty. Suspect anyone who approaches that jewel. Unfortunately, nothing will preserve it but downright force. Whenever you give up that force, you are ruined."

CHAPTER 24

"Lawful Money" vs. "Legal Tender"

The only thing you really need to know about economics is the law of supply and demand. When something is plentiful, the price tends to be very low due to lack of competition for the item. When something is scarce, the price increases accordingly because of the increased demand for it. That is why, over many centuries, and across numerous cultures, gold and silver have frequently been used as currency or a medium of exchange. Both of these metals are available in limited quantities, and have some intrinsic value of their own. Metals are also ductile and malleable which make it easy to stamp into consistent sizes and weights.

Still, the most important aspect of "money" is that it provides a convenient medium of exchange. We don't work hard because we like to collect paper dollars. We work for paper dollars because of all the luxuries and necessities we can exchange the paper dollars for. Occasionally people will refer to money as the "blood of the economy," and I think this is an excellent metaphor. If the doctor administers an intravenous medication, your blood pressure will slowly increase. If your blood pressure gets too high, it could be fatal. If the hospital staff mistakenly draws several pints of blood in the same hour, your blood pressure will drop, and you may not live long enough to complain. In order to maintain your health, your blood pressure must remain between a high and low danger level.

The same thing is true about money. If the volume of money increases or decreases beyond an acceptable limit, the economy begins to suffer.

Inflation is a condition defined by having too much currency in circulation. Imagine for a few moments that you are self-sufficient in nearly every way. The only commodity you need to buy or sell are bales of hay. It just so happens that there are *exactly* one million bales of hay available, and also *exactly* one million paper dollars in circulation. Given this convenient ratio, the cost of a bale of hay will be one dollar. Notice that the paper dollar has no intrinsic value, except that it can be traded for some hay. Through hard work and clever negotiation you manage to acquire one hundred bales of hay, however your one-room apartment does not provide enough space to store your hay. This is not a problem because you can trade your bales of hay and walk away with one hundred paper dollars. Eager to protect your savings, you place the dollars in your gun safe as you take out your trusty rifle. You lock the safe, turn on the perimeter alarm, and brew a pot of coffee to drink as you protect your hard-earned money all night.

During your nocturnal vigil, the Federal Reserve System prints another million paper dollars "out of thin air" and distributes them into the economy. As the sun comes up and you begin to think about breakfast, there are still one million bales of hay but now there are two million paper dollars to represent them. Because of the new ratio, the cost of a bale of hay will be *two* dollars. You open the safe to replace the rifle and grab the one hundred dollars you deposited there the night before. Unfortunately for you, your money will only buy *half* as many bales of hay as it used to. So, without triggering your alarm, walking past you and your dangerous rifle, or discovering the combination to your safe, the Federal Reserve has managed to steal half of your buying power. *That* is why inflation is bad.

Sometimes we are told that the inflation rate must remain at approximately 5 percent in order to maintain a healthy economy. Why do we accept that as true? If your doctor recommended that you gain 5 percent of your body weight each year, how long would it be before you were too heavy to get up off of the couch?

The opposite problem is deflation, which is an economic condition defined by a lack of sufficient currency in circulation. In October of 1929, the stock market experienced a catastrophic crash. That event marks the beginning of the Great Depression, however it was not the *cause* of the depression as most of us have been lead to believe. The Great Depression is characterized by almost universal unemployment and widespread hunger. Did the male population of the early 1930s suddenly go out on strike? Did husbands across the country tell their wives, "I think I have a vision problem. I just can't see going to work today." No! Of course not! Men were begging for jobs, selling pencils and apples on street corners in an effort to buy food for their children. So if it wasn't the stock market or an epidemic of laziness, exactly what did cause the Great Depression?

The depression was caused because the Federal Reserve deliberately contracted the money supply. By collecting all of their outstanding loans and refusing to make any more, money became extremely scarce. The day the stock market crashed in 1929, there was enough money in circulation so that every person in the United States could have $2,400 if evenly distributed. One year later there was less than $15 of currency in circulation per person. People couldn't buy food because there wasn't anything to exchange for it. Companies couldn't hire anyone because they had nothing to give them on payday. Imagine what would happen to your poker game if someone came by and took away all of the poker chips. You could shuffle the cards, but there wouldn't be any way to keep track of who was winning or losing.

Cheating people out of their money is not a new phenomenon. Here are some quotations that refer to this chronic problem.

"Of all contrivances for cheating the laboring classes of mankind, none has been more effective than that which deludes them with paper money."
—Daniel Webster

"All the perplexities, confusion and distress in America rise, not from defects in their Constitution or Confederation, not from want of honor or virtue, so much as from downright ignorance of the nature of coin, credit and circulation."
—John Adams, in a letter to Thomas Jefferson in 1787

"If the American people ever allow private banks to control the issue of their currency first by inflation and then by deflation, the banks and corporations

that will grow up around them will deprive the people of all property until their
children will wake up homeless on the continent their fathers conquered."

—Thomas Jefferson in 1802 in a letter to then
Secretary of the Treasury, Albert Gallatin

"Give me control over a nation's currency and I care not who makes its laws."

—Baron M. A. Rothschild (1744 - 1812)

For those who would like to continue researching this subject, I recommend the following book and videotape, both of which explain the creation of the Federal Reserve System: *The Creature from Jekell Island* by G. Edward Griffing (American Media, $20, ISBN 0-912986-21-2, www.RealityZone. com) and *The Money Masters—How International Bankers Gained Control Of America*, two three-hour videotapes (to order, call 1-888-THE-PLOT, extension 60, visit www.themoneymasters.com, or write Money Masters Video, Box 114, Piedmont, OK 73078).

CHAPTER 25

Corruption in the United States

"Power tends to corrupt, and absolute power corrupts absolutely. Great men are almost always bad men."[1]

—Lord Acton, in a letter to Bishop Mandell Creighton, 1887

The goal of the Continental Congress in 1787 was to grant the federal (soon to be national) government more power in such a way as to prevent the government from growing beyond the control of the citizens that it was intended to protect. The framers of the Constitution made the faulty assumption that We the People would keep close watch over the government because it was in our best interest to do so. I am ashamed to say that most Americans haven't got a clue about what the Constitution actually says. If We the People want to claim our rights, we must also claim final responsibility for what happens in Washington, D.C. If you vote for the "lesser of two evils" and your candidate wins, you still end up with evil.

Corruption in our government started even before the ink was dry on the Constitution. Alexander Hamilton was a nationalist who called himself a federalist. John Adams enacted the Alien and Sedition Act that made it illegal to publicly criticize the government. Andrew Jackson used "eminent domain" to justify American possession of Indian territory from a race of people who did not comprehend the idea of claiming air, water, or land as private property.

However the first president to blatantly violate the spirit of the Constitution was Abraham Lincoln. He was the first to misinterpret the Constitution in order to claim "extraordinary war powers." His quest was to keep the union together using whatever force was necessary. By what logic do you decide to save a nation by ignoring the principle that created it? Lincoln's motives may have been pure, but that does not absolve him from the crime of exceeding his limited executive powers.

Although Lincoln may have strayed from the Constitution, the president who gets my vote for most corrupt and evil is Franklin Delano Roosevelt. FDR used the panic of the Great Depression as a justification for establishing our deeply entrenched welfare system, which is "obviously" socialism to those of us who understand the sanctity of private property. He was the president who found a way to threaten the Supreme Court justices enough to make them reverse their decisions and bestow an aura of constitutionality on his theft-based program.

Whether you're giving out food stamps to the homeless, or government subsidies to large corporations, the welfare system in our country is based on theft. If someone confronts you with a gun in a dark alley and takes $100 of your money—that's theft. If the thief uses your $100 to purchase ice cream for the local orphans—it is still theft! The ends do not justify the means. Anytime your property (or money) is taken from you by force it is theft, even if it is the government doing the stealing. Rather than arguing whether the government has the power to collect income taxes, we should be questioning whether many of its bureaucratic agencies should exist in the first place. If we eliminate all of the unconstitutional agencies, the need for taxes will be practically nonexistent.

It has recently been documented that FDR not only knew about the attack on Pearl Harbor but that he also took deliberate steps to lure the Japanese into attacking our fleet.[2] Allow me to promote you to the rank of admiral. The Navy you command has two advantages. First: Moving targets are hard to hit, and all of your ships can zigzag at the first sign of trouble. Second: Your ships are even harder to find, because you are allowed to hide your ships anywhere in the Pacific Ocean, which is unimaginably vast. In the 1940s, without global positioning systems or spy satellites, even *you* don't know where your ships are unless they radioed home their position. You are about to make your first big decision as admiral. Do you think it is a good strategic maneuver to place all of your ships in one tiny harbor at the same time, and line them up in nice, neat rows?

Not even the lowliest bosun's mate with five minutes of training would be willing to follow through with such a plan. However FDR was a former secretary of the navy before he was elected to the White House. FDR fired at least one admiral because he refused to follow orders to dock the fleet in Hawaii. The Navy was deliberately made vulnerable to attack, and the Japanese were given every opportunity to take advantage of it. The results are recorded in history. For an American president to callously sacrifice the lives of thousands of sailors in order to gain public support for entry into World War II is an act of treason that deserves an eternity in hell, not a proud memorial in Washington.

Forty years after John F. Kennedy's assassination, we are still asked to believe that Lee Harvey Oswald was the lone gunman, and that the fatal shot was fired from behind. No one could watch the digitally enhanced sequence of the film taken by Abraham Zapruder in Dallas that November and deny that the fatal shot came from the front. I don't claim to know the truth behind that tragic event, but it is clear that the Warren Report is not an accurate analysis of what happened.

More recently, an FBI sniper killed the wife of Randy Weaver by shooting her through the head as she held their eighteen-month-old child in her arms. Mr. Weaver had relocated his family to live on an obscure mountain in Idaho because he didn't trust the government. They wanted to arrest him for sawing off a shotgun one-half inch shorter than allowed by law. For this crime, the government spent millions of dollars to monitor and then destroy his family. I can't imagine why Mr. Weaver didn't trust the government. (You're only paranoid if they're *not* out to get you.)

The Branch Davidians established a church in the quiet little community of Waco, Texas. Unfortunately for them, they had the "unmitigated gall" to shoot back when attacked and fired upon by Federal Bureau of Alcohol, Tobacco and Firearms agents who were attempting to justify government funding for their agency. It was alleged (but never proven) that children were being sexually abused by David Koresh. If this was true, then why not arrest Mr. Koresh during one of his frequent visits into town? Burning down the church they were trapped in certainly prevents anyone from molesting the children, but they may have preferred being alive.

Very little evidence was collected in Waco before the entire area was bulldozed as flat as a billiard table. The evidence that was collected was being stored at the FBI headquarters—in Oklahoma City. As the clamor to examine the evidence from Waco increased, that evidence suddenly became "unavailable" when an explosion destroyed part of the Murrah Federal Building. I have read a lot about the Oklahoma City bombing, and there are several things I don't understand. First, how could Timothy McVeigh's truck do so much damage to the Murrah Building on one side of the street, while leaving buildings on the other side of the street virtually untouched? Also, since McVeigh's truck was parked *outside* the building, why do photographs show so much debris scattered from the building *toward* the truck? Once again, I don't know what really happened in Oklahoma, but I have strong doubts about the government's official version of what happened.

I am not espousing any conspiracy theories, however I am old enough to know when people are lying to me. I think it is dangerous for Americans to leave their safety, and control of their economy, in the hands of people who are prone to prevarication.

CHAPTER 26

Is There Anything I Can Do About It?

People frequently ask me if I truly believe that I can make a differ-ence in the way our government works. There are only two possible answers to that question. If the answer is yes, then the sooner I start and the harder I work, the more of a difference I'll be able to make. If the answer is no, then our country has passed the point of no return on its way to becoming a totalitarian police state. I am too stubborn and optimistic to accept the second conclusion. Even if it is true, I refuse to sit here waiting for government agents to arrest me. The bad guys may win, but I'm going to make their lives as miserable as possible before I go. Patrick Henry understood that there are three possibilities:

1. You can live your life as a free sovereign.
2. You can die attempting to protect your freedom.
3. You can give up and succumb to slavery.

Patrick Henry and I refuse to be slaves. That is not an acceptable option. "I know not what course others may take, but as for me … Give me liberty, or give me death."

This book begins and ends with the same famous quote, which I hope lends it a sense of literary symmetry. If I have communicated some sense of my passion for liberty, then perhaps you understand the depth of my convictions when I repeat that phrase. I hope you are beginning to recognize legitimate threats to the freedoms that we so casually take for granted. Perhaps you're even beginning to share my passion for freedom. That is what it means to be an American patriot.

Many people will scorn this book because it suggests that life in the United States is not as rosy as we would like to believe. If my conclusions are true, then we are in very serious trouble and something must be done. It implies that *you* are going to have to leave your comfort zone and *do* something, taking actions to change the way our government operates. It is much easier to remain in denial so you won't be required to participate. I doubt that anyone in denial would have taken the time to read this far. So what *are* you going to do about it?

I am not advocating the use of violence except in self-defense. Only you can decide if there is "a clear and present danger" that justifies the use of force. I much prefer revolution to rebellion. In order to avoid a violent confrontation, I strongly advocate resistance to tyranny. We must be very vocal about it while we still have the opportunity to speak out about our oppressions. Talk to your friends and neighbors about politics and religion, *especially* if that labels you as a "terrorist." Reject the idea that those topics are inappropriate at social gatherings. Remember that this is an ideological war, so we need to fight against the words and ideas that threaten to deprive us of our property.

I am not advocating that you do anything in particular, however I hope that you will begin to do *something*. We the People have rights. We also have the responsibility of protecting those rights. Here are some suggestions for activism to get you started. I'm sure that a brief search of the Internet will uncover several other opportunities for you to express yourself. Get involved. Do it now.

The most important thing you can do is to educate yourself about what is going on. Compare what you've learned about the Constitution to the news reports that you watch each evening. This will undoubtedly take time and effort on your part. In the appendix I have included a list of books, videotapes, and audiotapes. There is no best place to start. Find something that interests you and get started.

You can join a political "third party" such as the Libertarian Party.[1] We Libertarians call ourselves "the party of principle," insisting that you are free to do anything you want as long as you do not initiate force against another person or another person's property. People sometimes complain that "Libertarian candidates all sound alike." Why is that a bad thing? If I see a Libertarian candidate on the ballot, I know that candidate wants a much smaller government, he or she is pro-Second Amendment, and he or she opposes the loss of liberties caused by the war on drugs. You cannot make a similar claim about a Republican or Democratic candidate with whom you are unfamiliar. It is impossible to know where their candidates stand on an issue until they address it. Even then, their answers tend to be ambiguous, and are likely to contradict something they've said on a previous occasion. The good news is that joining the Libertarian Party does not prevent you from voting for someone else if you are still convinced that you will be wasting your vote. However by joining the party, you are still sending a message to Congress that you will not tolerate further violations of your rights.

You can help return America to value, "one dollar at a time" by becoming a Liberty Associate, and using a new silver-based currency called the Liberty Dollar.[2] This is private money that is 100 percent backed by substance, in contrast to the debt-based fiat currency provided by the Federal Reserve System. Offering merchants the Liberty Dollar helps raise awareness of the runaway inflation of our economy, and gives us a non-violent method of changing the system. You can also create gold-based accounts on the Internet that allow you to purchase items and services from pro-liberty merchants. Very soon it will be possible to do all of your business privately and secretly using secure servers on the Internet. When that happens, the Federal Reserve will collapse from lack of use.

You can learn more about our convoluted and corrupted system of laws by joining the Fully Informed Jury Association (FIJA).[3] It provides information to prospective jurors explaining that they have the power to judge the law as well as the facts of a case—contradicting the jury instructions typically given by a judge. There are also many good books about common law that will explain the jurisdiction our courts used to respect. Hopefully they will do so again in the future.

If you can find an honest candidate you trust, offer to volunteer for his or her campaign. Better yet, you can run for office yourself. It's not as difficult to get started as you think, and you will quickly dispel any feelings of helplessness brought about by your lack of action.

For those who are willing to "vote with your feet," the Free State Project has recently selected New Hampshire as the place where 20,000 liberty-loving activists will move in an effort to change the state through the legislative process.[4] I am proud to be among the first 5,000 to join the movement, recognizing that "something must be done," and that I am one of the people who will do it.

And for the most radical of readers, there are even a few groups, especially in Hawaii and Texas, who are talking seriously about seceding from the union. A group of Texans has gone so far as to write the Texas Constitution 2000 (known as TC2K).[5] I have read this Constitution and believe it to be even better than the federal/national Constitution we have just studied.

We have come to the final chapter of this study of our government, the Constitution and what I believe about liberty. As an instructor, I hope you have found it both enjoyable and enlightening. If you feel a more personal connection to the documents that define our great nation, then my goal has been achieved. I will be using this book as the text of an eight-hour class that I will continue to present until I discover a more effective way to promote the ideals that our founders left to us. You can find out more about my class by visiting my web site.[6] In the meantime, I leave you with a quote from Thomas Paine, who wrote this for George Washington to read to his troops at Valley Forge.

"These are the times that try men's souls. The summer soldier and the sunshine patriot will, in this crisis, shrink from the service of their country; but he that stands it now, deserves the love and thanks of man and woman. Tyranny, like hell, is not easily conquered; yet we have this consolation with us, that the harder the conflict, the more glorious the triumph."

—Thomas Paine

APPENDIX

Books

The Federalist Papers. A collection of newspaper articles written (under pseud-onym) by Alexander Hamilton, James Madison, and John Jay promoting the ratification of the Constitution. ISBN 0-451-62541-2 / published by Mentor / $6.00

The Anti-Federalist Papers. A lesser-known collection of newspaper articles written, in part, by Patrick Henry and John DeWitt, expressing concern about forming a strong central government. ISBN 0-451-62525-0 / published by Mentor / $7.00

A Familiar Exposition of the Constitution of the United States. Written by U.S. Supreme Court Justice Joseph Story in 1840. Story was born in 1779, just three years after the signing of the Declaration of Independence. He served on the Supreme Court from 1811 until his death in 1845. He understood that the Constitution is meaningless unless it is rigorously defended by citizens who understand the original intentions of the men who drafted the docu-ment. ISBN 0-89526-796-9 / published by Regnery Gateway

The History of American Constitutional or Common Law with Commentary Concerning Equity and Merchant Law. Written by Dale Pond, Howard Fisher, Richard Knutson, and the North American Freedom Council. This book explains common law, equity law, and admiralty law, and explains the basis of the Uniform Commercial Code. It also discusses the issue of sovereignty and the difference between state citizens and United States citizens. ISBN 1-57282-010-1 / published by the Message Company / $12.00

The Common Law of the United States of America of the Sovereign People. Written and compiled by Jerry Henson. This book explains common law, equity law, and admiralty law, and explains the basis of the Uniform Commercial Code. It also discusses the issue of sovereignty and the difference between state citizens and United States citizens. "We are not a democracy. We are a republic form of government with all of the checks and balances needed to prevent government from usurping our constitutionally guaranteed rights." Published by Lighthouse Color Press / POB 15742 / Del City [73155] Oklahoma

The Global Sovereign's Handbook. The most comprehensive sourcebook on sovereignty available anywhere in the world. This all-new edition specifically designed and packaged for the global sovereign—people committed to freedom and justice for all the people of the world, regardless of race, class, creed or color. no ISBN / published by CRC / $105. www.cascadian.com/CRC/Products/GSHHome.html

The Sovereign Individual. How to Survive and Thrive during the Collapse of the Welfare State. Written by James Dale Davidson and Lord William Rees-Mogg. In previous books these authors accurately predicted the end of communism, the dissolution of the Soviet Union, and the bankruptcies of American Savings and Loan associations. ISBN 0-684-81007-7 / published by Simon and Schuster / $25.00

The Creature from Jekell Island. Written by G. Edward Griffin to describe the creation of the Federal Reserve Bank in 1913. Mr. Griffin asserts that it should be abolished because "It is incapable of accomplishing its stated objectives. It is a cartel operating against the public interest. It is the supreme instrument of usury. It generates our most unfair tax. It encourages war. It destabilizes the economy. It is an instrument of totalitarianism." ISBN 0-912986-21-2 / published by American Media / $20.00

The Fourteenth Amendment and the Bill of Rights. Written by Raoul Berger, this book questions whether or not the Bill of Rights applies to the states by virtue of the Fourteenth Amendment. If it doesn't, many modern decisions of the Supreme Court are without constitutional warrant. It establishes the fact that the Fourteenth Amendment formally adopted civil rights laws that were written for the purpose of controlling the recently repatriated Southern states. ISBN 0-8061-2186-6 / published by University of Oklahoma Press / $25.00

Unintended Consequences. Written by John Ross, this book is a beautiful blend of historical facts and hypothetical fiction. I *loved* this book. It has been described as "the *Atlas Shrugged* of the gun culture." Very recently the ATF department has be flagrantly harassing Mr. Ross by pressuring his estranged wife to testify against him on federal charges. ISBN 1-888-11804-0 / published by Accurate Press / $30.00

The Samurai, the Mountie, and the Cowboy: Should America Adopt the Gun Controls of Other Democracies? [sic]. Written by David R. Kopel. I thought this was an excellent book for understanding why different cultures have vastly different approaches to violence. Anti-gun proponents frequently point to Japan as a model of gun-free safety—overlooking the fact that Japanese citizens have no rights, and do not expect any because they willingly accept a paternalistic, omnipotent government. In contrast, Switzerland trains every adult male how to use a large-caliber, fully automatic rifle. As a result, Switzerland has *no crime*, and can mobile 240,000 armed troops in twenty-four hours! ISBN 0-87975-756-6 / published by Prometheus Books / $37.00

Hologram of Liberty—The Constitution's Shocking Alliance with Big Government. Written by Kenneth W. Royce (a.k.a. Boston T Party), this book is only recommended for "advanced study," because it suggests the Constitution is flawed by deliberate design. If you are still having trouble accepting the idea that the folks in Washington, D.C., are *not* on your side, then you are not quite ready for this, yet. ISBN 1-888766-03-4 / published by Javelin Press (in *Austin, Texas!*) / $19.95. www.javelinpress.com

Lost Rights—The Destruction of American Liberty. Written by James Bovard. You cannot read this book and maintain your blissful naiveté about government corruption. This book made me so angry I had to read it one chapter at a time. It contains descriptions of a San Diego drug bust where the police raided a family at two o'clock in the morning and held a .45-caliber gun to the head of a six-year-old boy. It also recounts an attempt by the IRS to extract taxes from a Michigan daycare center—by holding the young children hostage until their parents signed documents assuming liability for the (presumed) debt. This is a must-read book. ISBN 0-312-12333-7 / published by St. Martin's Griffin / $17.00

"feeling your pain"—The Explosion and Abuse of government power in the Clinton-Gore Years. Written by James Bovard, this book is a great "sequel" to Lost Rights.. ISBN 0-312-23082-6 / published by St. Martin's Press / $27.00

Economics in One Lesson. Written by Henry Hazlitt, this small paperback takes only five pages to explain how economics *should* work. The rest of the book is dedicated to understanding various problems in America that are created because our economy *doesn't* work that way. ISBN 0-517-54823-2 / published by Crown Publishers / $10.00

The Communist Manifesto. Written by Karl Marx and Friedrich Engels in 1848 to outline what "the perfect communist society would look like." Marx recognized the power of capitalism, but he felt that it would destroy society. Although he claimed that "the workers have nothing to lose but their chains," this book describes the ideology that turns men into slaves. "Know thy enemy!" ISBN 1-85984-898-2 / published by Verso (London) / $20.00

Our Enemy The State. Written by Albert Jay Nock in 1935. The theme of the book is State Power versus Social Power and the "political means" versus the "economic means" as this struggle has taken place throughout the history of the United States, from the Colonial days up into the New Deal of Franklin D. Roosevelt. ISBN 0-930073-04-5 / published by Fox and Wilkes

The Discovery of Freedom. Written by Rose Wilder Lane in 1943. She summarily indicts Old World thinkers for holding to the ancient belief that some authority always controls the individual. For Rose Wilder Lane, the history of mankind could be understood only as the theater of two diverse forces, the authoritarians and the revolutionists, locked in an unending struggle for supremacy. ISBN 0-930073-00-2 / published by Fox and Wilkes

101 Things to Do 'Til the Revolution—Ideas and Resources for Self-Liberation. Written by Claire Wolfe, published in January 1999. She says, "America is at that awkward stage. It's too late to work within the system, but too early to shoot the bastards." She has grasped the current stage of our struggle: firm mental defiance coupled with the beginning of real action. ISBN 1-89362-613-X / published by Loompanics Unlimited / $15.95

Don't Shoot the Bastards (Yet)—101 More Ways to Salvage Freedom. Written by Claire Wolfe, published in April 1999. This is a follow-up to her earlier book, *101 Things to Do Until the Revolution.* It covers the same themes, but contains all new material. ISBN 1-55950-189-8 / published by Loompanics Unlimited / $15.95

Videotapes

1776. This is a wonderful musical (knowledge is not necessarily boring) that depicts the heated debates that led to the signing of the Declaration of Independence, which occurs just before the closing credits. I sincerely doubt that our Founding Fathers broke into song, but I feel very strongly that every other detail is historically correct. You can easily rent this from Blockbuster or other video store. (148 minutes). ISBN 0-8001-0657-1

Liberty. This is an excellent dramatic recreation of the American Revolution. Numerous actors and actresses portray famous characters, so you can watch the war "as it happens." Watching this PBS Home Video series is even better than having been there—because the chances of giving your life for liberty is extremely low while sitting on the living room sofa. The haunting music from this video is also available separately on audiotape. (3 tapes / 6 hours). ISBN 0-7806-2013-5

The American Revolution. This series is a narrated documentary produced by The History Channel and A&E Home Network. If your high school civics class was this good, you would never have forgotten the principles of our republican government. (6 tapes / 50 minutes each). ISBN 1-56501-436-7

The Money Masters—How International Bankers Gained Control of America. You *must* watch this video! It begins with an explanation of how ancient goldsmiths invented fractional reserve banking, and how the privately owned Bank of England established power over the king himself. Learn how private central banks have been established and overthrown here in the United States—until the Federal Reserve was created in 1913. This is an excellent video to watch if you don't have the patience to read *The Creature from Jekyll Island.* (2 tapes / 3 hours). To order call 1-888-THE-PLOT, ext. 60, or write Money Masters Video, Box 114, Piedmont, OK 73078

The NORFED Solution: An Introduction to the American Liberty Dollar. This is a video of a presentation given by Bernard von NotHaus, the founder of NORFED, to a receptive audience in Las Vegas on May 7, 2000. (65 minutes). To order call 1-888-421-6181 or go to www.norfed.org/

Waco: The Rules of Engagement. You will never feel the same way about the U.S. government after watching this video. This is not an angry, biased denunciation of the ATF and FBI. It is a collection of interviews and raw data and video taken by the ATF and FBI as it happened. You are simply presented with the information and allowed to form your own opinion. I don't think you can rent this, so you'll probably have to buy or borrow it. (136 minutes). www.waco93.com/

The People's Century—Ordinary People, Extraordinary Times. This is an excellent twenty-six-hour college telecourse presented by PBS and WGBH/Boston. Although it is available at www.pbs.org/, unfortunately I don't think you can buy the tapes individually. The first set is a series of fourteen tapes for $170.00 I will not loan out tapes from my video library, but I would consider showing them to an interested group at my home. The six episodes I would recommend are:

Age of Hope—Optimism Reigns as the New Century Begins. ISBN 1-57807-105-4

Killing Fields—The First World War. ISBN 1-57807-115-1

Red Flag—Communism in Russia. ISBN 1-57807-120-8

Brave New World—The Cold War Begins. ISBN 1-57807-107-0

Freedom Now—Colonial Rule is Overthrown in India and Africa. ISBN 1-57807-111-9

People Power—The End of Soviet Style Communism. ISBN 1-57807-119-4

America Rock. Part of the Schoolhouse Rock! series, this is a great children's video (that many adults could probably learn from) that features great animated features with easy to remember songs—most notably "The Preamble." If you can't learn the preamble to the Constitution singing this little song, you are in deep trouble. ISBN 1-56949-408-8 / $17.00

Knowledge Equals Freedom (Volume 1). Produced by Dennis Grover, American. This is an excellent series of short clips from his weekly television show, "Liberty and Justice for All," covering topics such as the government-controlled media and the ongoing "land grab" by the National Forest Service. (You really *must see* the segment titled "Big Park.") (2 hours). www.knowfree.com/vidone.htm / $20.00 plus shipping

Badnarik on the 10 Planks of the Communist Manifesto. Michael Badnarik talks about the difference between rights and privileges and the difference between a democracy and a republic. He then goes on to outline each of the ten planks of the *Communist Manifesto*, showing how each plank is being implemented here in the United States. How do you like living in a communist country? (1 hour) www.ConstitutionPreservation.org / $10.00 plus $2.00 for shipping. www.realityexpander.com/

Audiotapes

Constitution series. These tapes are from a series by Knowledge Products, available at Barnes & Noble: "Narrated by Walter Cronkite, these cassettes take you back to Philadelphia in 1787—to four months filled with back-room deals, political scheming and fierce debates. You'll feel the full impact of conflicts and passions that nearly tore apart the Philadelphia Convention, the ratification process, and the infant American nation. You'll understand the Constitution in a way you've never known before." (This is *mandatory* listening.). Each audiobook contains two tapes, lasts three hours, and costs $18.00 or you can order the entire set for only $51.00 from www.audioclassics.net/html/con_files/const.htm

The Constitutional Convention. The Text of the Constitution The Ratification Debates The Bill of Rights and other Amendments also recommended, but not officially part of the above series *The Federalist Papers*

The Declaration of Independence. This lecture by John Ridpath examines the historical background of the decade prior to 1776; the process by which the Declaration was written and ratified; and the subsequent fate of both the Declaration and some of its heroic signers. (1 tape / 90 minutes). available from Second Renaissance Books / $12.95 / www.secondrenaissance.com / (800) 729-6149

An Historical Perspective on Revolution. This lecture by George H. Smith was presented at the 1996 ISIL World Conference in Whistler, British Columbia, Canada. Smith demonstrates, in a very convincing manner, that our Founding Fathers were attempting to establish a very *limited* federal government. (1 tape / 60 minutes) . available from International Society for Individual Liberty / $11.95. 836-B Southampton Road, No. 299, Benicia, CA 94510 / (707) 746-8796

The Spirit of 1776—Inspiration from Patrick Henry, Thomas Jefferson & Others. Bruce Evoy does an *excellent* job of narrating such things as Patrick Henry's "give me liberty or give me death" speech and "the midnight ride of Paul Revere." When you hear him recite the Declaration of Independence, it really seems to hit home. (1 tape / 60 minutes). available from International Society for Individual Liberty / $11.95. 836-B Southampton Road, No. 299, Benicia, CA 94510 / (707) 746-8796

How Tyranny Came to America. Joseph Sobran is a nationally syndicated writer. This relatively short tape describes the slow and imperceptible changes that have been made to our Constitution throughout its history. This is an *excellent* "first tape" for any of your friends and relatives that consider you "an extremist and a radical." (My mother *loved* it!). (1 tape / 40 minutes) Sobran's, 713 Park Street SE, Vienna, VA 22180 / $6.00. www.sobran.com to order the tape. www.sobran.com/tyranny.shtml to read the text of the tape for free.

The following tapes are available at www.realityzone.com/ from the "Audio Archives." Each volume contains three audiotapes and cost $15.00 in you order from the Internet. These tapes can also be purchased individually for $8.00 if you order on the internet. "Zone Dwellers are not content to *acquire* information; their mission is to share it. As long as you are a subscriber, you will have the right to make unlimited copies of any tape to give to your friends, so long as the copies are given, not sold, and no material is added or deleted, including announcements at the beginning and end." The tapes I strongly recommend are in bold.

Volume 1. **The Creature from Jekyll Island; A Second Look at the Federal Reserve.** MacArthur's Farewell Address / **Sockdolager!** (Davey Crocket) Natural Progesterone, the Amazing Hormone

Volume 2. **The Hidden Agenda** (testimony of Norman Dodd regarding tax exempt organizations)

The Law (Frederic Bastiat exposes the contradictions of socialism)

World Without Cancer; The Story of Vitamin B17 (Laetrile)

Volume 3. **Lesson from Austria** (Kitty Werthman describes Hitler's rise to power in Austria)

The Politics of Cancer Therapy

I was a spy for Joseph Stalin (the testimony of Alexander Contract)

Volume 4. **Mind Control, The Ultimate Weapon** (lecture by Major William Mayer about the Korean War—the first time in history that American prisoners never tried to escape)

Why We Need Separation of School and State (How and why government schools are twisting the minds of our kids)

The Perfect Tax (An address by G. Edward Griffin)

ENDNOTES

Preface

1. www.brainyquote.com/quotes/authors/d/danielwebs126392.html.

2. www.lexrex.com/enlightened/AmericanIdeal/intro_quotes.html.

3. "If ye love wealth greater than liberty, the tranquility of servitude greater than the animating contest for freedom, go home from us in peace. We seek not your counsel nor your arms. Crouch down and lick the hand that feeds you and may posterity forget that ye were once our countrymen."—Samuel Adams

Chapter 1

1. These documents are known as the "Dunlap broadsides" named after the printer who made them. Only twenty-five are known to have survived until today.

2. Visit www.ArticlesOfConfederation.org to learn more about George Washington's predecessors.

3. *Webster's New Collegiate Dictionary*, 1981, page 562.

4. Paul Begala, an advisor to the Clinton White House, is quoted as saying, "Stroke of the pen. Law of the land. Kinda cool!"

5. A table on page 1651 of *Black's Law Dictionary* (Rev 6) shows the complete history of the Supreme Court. The number of justices on the court in a given year is summarized here, with nine being the most stable number since 1870: Five in 1789. Six in 1790. Seven in 1807. Nine in 1837. Eight in 1844. Nine in 1846. Eight in 1861. Nine in 1862. Ten in 1863. Nine in 1866. Eight in 1867. Nine in 1870. Eight in 1969. Nine in 1970. Seven in 1971. Nine since 1972.

Chapter 2

1. www.ConstitutionPreservation.org.

2. *Black's Law Dictionary*, 6th Edition, page 1325.

3. ibid., page 1197.

4. www.ejfi.org/Courts/Courts-2.htm.

5. Speech, Osawatomie, August 31, 1910, (Edmund Morris, *The Rise Of Theodore Roosevelt,* Modern Library 2001).

6. www.nationalatlas.gov/fedlandsprint.html. "The Federal Government owns nearly 650 million acres of land—almost 30 percent of the land area of the United States."

Chapter 3

1. *Black's Law Dictionary*, 6th Edition, page 1140.

2. ibid., page 919.

3. ibid., page 973.

4. ibid., page 815.

5. ibid., page 999.

6. www.indystar.com/library/factfiles/religion/churches/baptist_temple/tax_dispute.html.

7. *Black's Law Dictionary*, 6th Edition, page 920.

8. ibid., page 1495.

9. ibid., page 269.

10. ibid., page 1499.

11. ibid., page 214.

12. ibid., page 1123.

13. ibid., page 1554.

Chapter 4

1. *Black's Law Dictionary*, 6th Edition, page 1395.

2. www.bartleby.com/100/248.6.html.

3. www.quotedb.com/quotes/2074.

4. www.senate.gov/~rpc/releases/1999/gc012901.htm (March 4, 1861).

5. www.brainyquote.com/quotes/authors/a/abrahamlin125100.html (February 12, 1865).

6. www.RealityZone.com, Audio Archive. Lesson from Austria (Kitty Werthman describes Hitler's rise to power in Austria). www.us-israel.org/jsource/Holocaust/kristallnacht.html. "So, it appears, the term 'Kristallnacht' or 'Crystal Night' was invented by Nazis to mock Jews on that black November night in 1938."

Chapter 5

1. Washington's presidential farewell address, January 7, 1790.

2. A government or state in which the supreme power is actually or nominally lodged in a monarch. A monarch is defined as "a hereditary sovereign as a king, queen, or emperor; the sole and absolute ruler of a state."

3. A form of government in which the power is vested in a few persons or in a dominant class or clique; a government by the few.

4. A form of government in which the supreme power is vested in the people and exercised directly by them or by their elected agents.

5. www.bartleby.com/73/424.html. Attributed to Alexander Fraser Tytler, Lord Woodhouselee. Unverified.

6. *Webster's New Collegiate Dictionary*, 1981, page 1094.

7. ibid., page 226.

Chapter 7

1. *The Founding Fathers*, a PBS videotape series.

2. *Webster's New Collegiate Dictionary*, 1981, page 416.

3. ibid., page 758.

Chapter 9

1. An audiotape series from Knowledge Products titled *The Constitutional Convention, The Text of the Constitution, The Ratification Debates,* and *The Bill of Rights and other Amendments.* You can find them at www.audioclassics.net/html/con_files/const.htm.

2. Reported by the Associated Press on Sunday, September 14, 2003, in an article titled "Poll suggests public opposition to additional $87 billion for Iraq." This article was posted at www.newsobserver.com/24hour/special_reports/iraq/homefront/story/998533p-7011246c.html.

3. This assumes a U.S. population of 285 million.

4. From an article titled "Constitutional Economics 101: What is a Dollar?" by Dr. Judd W. Patton, found at academic.bellevue.edu/~jpatton/print/dollar.html.

5. "The Creature from Jekyle Island" by G. Edward Griffin.

6. Black on Constitutional Law 1910 3d edition p274—Letters of Marque. A letter of marque is a commission given to a private ship by a government to make reprisals on the ships of another government. The power to grant letters of marque is incidental and implied in the power to declare war. But it is also sometimes resorted to, not as a measure of hostility, but rather as a peace measure, and is intended to prevent the necessity of other or more extreme acts of hostility. It was therefore properly specified as one of the enumerated powers of congress, instead of being left to be inferred from the more general grant of authority to declare war.

7. *Webster's New Collegiate Dictionary* (1981), page 723.

8. "The Samurai, the Mountie, and the Cowboy," written by David R. Kopel and published by Prometheus Books ISBN 0-87975-756-6.

9. More formally known as the "Uniting and Strengthening America by Providing Appropriate Tools Required to Intercept and Obstruct Terrorism (USA PATRIOT ACT) Act of 2001".

10. Section 213 of the Patriot Act, entitled "Authority For Delaying Notice Of The Execution Of A Warrant".

11. *Black's Law Dictionary*, 6th Edition, page 126.

12. ibid., page 580.

Chapter 10

1. www.lp.org/campaigns/pres/.

2. *Black's Law Dictionary*, 6th Edition, page 709.

Chapter 11

1. *Black's Law Dictionary*, 6th Edition, page 276.

2. ibid., page 540.

3. ibid., page 47.

4. ibid., page 969.

5. from personal e-mail correspondence with Rick Stanley, although these comments have been posted on the internet.

6. *Black's Law Dictionary*, 6th Edition, page 1412.

7. ibid., page 1410.

8. ibid., page 1531.

Chapter 12

1. *Crosse v. Board of Supervisors of Elections*, (221 A.2d. 431 1966).

2. *Black's Law Dictionary*, 6th Edition, page 1142.

3. ibid., page 340.

4. This refers to a form of government that respects and protects individual rights. It does not refer to political party represented by an elephant.

Chapter 13

1. abcnews.go.com/sections/us/DailyNews/alaska_patriot030523.html *and* www.americanfreepress.net/04_26_03/Patriot_Rebellion/patriot_rebellion.html.

Chapter 14

1. Patrick Henry during the Virginia Ratifying Convention, June 5, 1788.

2. "The poorest man may, in his cottage, bid defiance to all the forces of the Crown. It may be frail; its roof may shake; the wind may blow through it; the storms may enter; the rain may enter; but the King of England cannot enter; all his forces dare not cross the threshold of the ruined tenement."— William Pitt.

Chapter 15

1. www.lexrex.com/enlightened/AmericanIdeal/intro_quotes.html.

2. www.givemeliberty.org.

Chapter 18

1. www.fija.org.

2. *Black's Law Dictionary*, 6th Edition, page 354.

3. ibid., page 523.

Chapter 21

1. *Black's Law Dictionary*, 6th Edition, page 211.

2. ibid., page 461.

3. *McCulloch v. Maryland*, 4 Wheat. 431 (1819), Marshall, C.J.

4. *Black's Law Dictionary*, 6th Edition, page 773.

5. www.thelawthatneverwas.com/.

6. These questions were generated by Larkin Rose whose web site is taxableincome.net. He also has an excellent videotape that explains who is (and is not) liable to pay the federal/national income tax. Those can be purchased at www.theft-by-deception.com. You can also visit www.861.info.

Chapter 22

1. www.urbanlegends.com/legal/pi_indiana.html.

2. This is an example of sarcasm.

3. users.rcn.com/virtual.nai/sot/videos/obstruct.htm.

Chapter 25

1. phrases.shu.ac.uk/meanings/22900.html.

2. *Day of Deceit—The Truth about FDR and Pearl Harbor*, by Robert B. Stinnett (ISBN 0-684-85339-6).

Chapter 26

1. www.LP.org.

2. www.LibertyDollar.org.

3. www.FIJA.org.

4. www.FreeStateProject.org.

5. www.FreeTexans.org.

6. www.ConstitutionPreservation.org.

CONSTITUTIONAL QUIZ

1. What type of government does the Constitution create for the United States? _____

    a) monarchy   *c) democracy*   *e) other*

    b) oligarchy   *d) plutocracy*

2. The Declaration of Independence marks the beginning of the Revolutionary War. Which document marks the END of the Revolutionary War? _____

    a) Articles of Confederation   *d) Treaty of Versaillese*

    b) Constitution   *e) Federalist Papers*

    c) Treaty of Paris

3. In what year did the framers <u>sign</u> the Constitution? _____

    a) 1776   *c) 1789*   *e) none of the above*

    b) 1787   *d) 1791*

4. How many states had to ratify the Constitution before it was instituted as "the supreme law of the land"? _____

    a) six   *c) ten*   *e) all thirteen*

    b) nine   *d) twelve*

5. Which of these famous documents includes a preamble? _____

    a) only the Declaration of Independence

    b) only the Constitution

    c) the Declaration of Independence and the Constitution

    d) the Constitution and the Bill of Rights

    e) the Preamble is a separate document

6. Which Article of the Constitution establishes a minimum age for senators and members of the House of Representatives? _____

    a) Article I   *c) Article III*   *e) no age requirement*
    b) Article II   *d) Article V*

7. The president of the United States takes an oath of office at his inauguration. Which article of the Constitution establishes the text of this oath? _____

    a) Article I   *c) Article III*   *e) it is not explicitly listed*
    b) Article II   *d) Article V*

8. Article III of the Constitution establishes the judiciary branch of our government. How many forms of law is the Supreme Court authorized to preside over? _____

    a) one: the Constitution is the supreme (and only) law of the land
    b) two   *d) four*
    c) three   *e) none*

9. Which of the following IS NOT enacted by Article IV of the Constitution? _____

    a) full faith and credit shall be extended by each state to every other state
    b) each state may claim its own citizens
    c) criminals must be returned to the state where they are convicted of a crime
    d) new states may be added to the union
    e) any person born or naturalized in the U.S. is a citizen of the United States

10. What percentage of Congress is necessary to propose an amendment the Constitution? _____

    a) 51%   *c) 75%*   *e) none of the above*
    b) 66.6%   *d) 80%*

11. What percentage of the states are necessary to ratify a proposed amendment? _____

    a) 51%   *c) 75%*   *e) none of the above*
    b) 66.6%   *d) 80%*

12. Which of the following rights are granted to you by the Bill of Rights? _____

    a) no soldiers in your home   *d) all of the above*
    b) no excessive bail   *e) none of the above*
    c) keep and bear arms

13. Which amendment requires a warrant to be supported by oath or affirmation? _____

    a) First Amendment   *d) Sixth Amendment*

    b) Second Amendment   *e) none of the above*

    c) Fourth Amendment

14. Which amendment protects your right to a speedy and public trial?
_____

    a) Third Amendment   *d) Eighth Amendment*

    b) Fifth Amendment   *e) none of the above*

    c) Sixth Amendment

15. Which amendment speaks of petitioning the government for a redress of grievances? _____

    a) First Amendment   *d) Tenth Amendment*

    b) Fifth Amendment   *e) none of the above*

    c) Ninth Amendment

16. Which amendment protects the right of the National Guard to keep and bear arms? _____

    a) First Amendment   *d) Sixth Amendment*

    b) Second Amendment   *e) none of the above*

    c) Fourth Amendment

17. Which amendment refers to a tax on "income from any source derived"? _____

    a) Fourteenth Amendment   *d) Twenty-First Amendment*

    b) Sixteenth Amendment   *e) Twenty-Fifth Amendment*

    c) Eighteenth Amendment

18 . Which amendment started the prohibition of alcohol in the United States? _____

    a) Fourteenth Amendment   *d) Twenty-First Amendment*

    b) Sixteenth Amendment   *e) Twenty-Fifth Amendment*

    c) Eighteenth Amendment

19. Which amendment stopped the prohibition of alcohol in the United States? _____

    a) Fourteenth Amendment   *d) Twenty-First Amendment*

    b) Sixteenth Amendment   *e) Twenty-Fifth Amendment*

    c) Eighteenth Amendment

20. What year was the last time the Constitution was amended? _____

    a) 1913   *c) 1951*   *e) 1992*

    b) 1933   *d) 1961*

The unanimous Declaration of the thirteen united States of America

When in the Course of human events, it becomes necessary for one people to dissolve the political bands which have connected them with another, and to assume among the Powers of the earth, the separate and equal station to which the Laws of Nature and of Nature's God entitle them, a decent respect to the opinions of mankind requires that they should declare the causes which impel them to the separation.

We hold these truths to be self-evident, that all men are created equal, that they are endowed by their Creator with certain unalienable Rights, that among these are Life, Liberty and the pursuit of Happiness.

That to secure these rights, Governments are instituted among Men, deriving their just powers from the consent of the governed.

That whenever any Form of Government becomes destructive of these ends, it is the Right of the People to alter or to abolish it, and to institute new Government, laying its foundation on such principles and organizing its powers in such form, as to them shall seem most likely to effect their Safety and Happiness. Prudence, indeed, will dictate that Governments long established should not be changed for light and transient causes; and accordingly all experience hath shown, that mankind are more disposed to suffer, while evils are sufferable, than to right themselves by abolishing the forms to which they are accustomed. But when a long train of abuses and usurpations, pursuing invariably the same Object, evinces a design to reduce them under absolute Despotism, it is their right, it is their duty, to throw off such Government, and to provide new Guards for their future security.

Such has been the patient sufferance of these Colonies; and such is now the necessity which constrains them to alter their former Systems of Government. The history of the present King of Great Britain is a history of repeated injuries and usurpations, all having in direct object the establishment of an absolute Tyranny over these States. To prove this, let Facts be submitted to a candid world.

He has refused his Assent to Laws, the most wholesome and necessary for the public good.

He has forbidden his Governors to pass Laws of immediate and pressing importance, unless suspended in their operation till his Assent should be obtained; an when so suspended, he has utterly neglected to attend to them.

He has refused to pass other Laws for the accommodation of large districts of people, unless those people would relinquish the right of Representation in the Legislature, a right inestimable to them and formidable to tyrants only.

He has called together legislative bodies at places unusual, uncomfortable, and distant from the depository of their public Records, for the sole purpose of fatiguing them into compliance with his measures.

He has dissolved Representative Houses repeatedly, for opposing with manly firmness his invasions on the rights of the people.

He has refused for a long time, after such dissolutions, to cause others to be elected; whereby the Legislative powers, incapable of Annihilation, have returned to the People at large for their exercise; the State remaining in the mean time exposed to all the dangers of invasion from without, and convulsions within.

He has endeavoured to prevent the population of these States; for that purpose obstructing the Laws of Naturalization of Foreigners; refusing to pass others to encourage their migrations hither, and raising the conditions of new Appropriations of Lands.

He has obstructed the Administration of Justice, by refusing his Assent to Laws for establishing Judiciary powers.

He has made Judges dependent on his Will alone, for the tenure of their offices, and the amount and payment of their salaries.

He has erected a multitude of New Offices, and sent hither swarms of Officers to harass our People, and eat out their substance.

He has kept among us, in times of peace, Standing Armies without the Consent of our legislatures.

He has affected to render the Military independent of and superior to the Civil power.

He has combined with others to subject us to a jurisdiction foreign to our constitution, and unacknowledged by our laws; giving his Assent to their Acts of pretended Legislation:

For quartering large bodies of armed troops among us:

For protecting them, by a mock Trial, from Punishment for any Murders which they should commit on the Inhabitants of these States:

For cutting off our Trade with all parts of the world:

For imposing Taxes on us without our Consent:

For depriving us in many cases, of the benefits of Trial by Jury:

For transporting us beyond Seas to be tried for pretended offences:

For abolishing the free System of English Laws in a neighbouring Province, establishing therein an Arbitrary government, and enlarging its Boundaries so as to render it at once an example and fit instrument for introducing the same absolute rule into these Colonies:

For taking away our Charters, abolishing our most valuable Laws, and altering fundamentally the Forms of our Governments:

For suspending our own Legislatures, and declaring themselves invested with power to legislate for us in all cases whatsoever.

He has abdicated Government here, by declaring us out of his Protection and waging War against us.

He has plundered our seas, ravaged our Coasts, burnt our towns, and destroyed the Lives of our people.

He is at this time transporting large armies of foreign mercenaries to compleat the works of death, desolation and tyranny, already begun with circumstances of Cruelty & perfidy scarcely paralleled in the most barbarous ages, and totally unworthy the Head of a civilized nation.

He has constrained our fellow Citizens taken Captive on the high Seas to bear Arms against their Country, to become the executioners of their friends and Brethren, or to fall themselves by their Hands.

He has excited domestic insurrections amongst us, and has endeavoured to bring on the inhabitants of our frontiers, the merciless Indian Savages, whose known rule of warfare, is an undistinguished destruction of all ages, sexes and conditions.

In every stage of these Oppressions We have Petitioned for Redress in the most humble terms: Our repeated Petitions have been answered only by repeated injury. A Prince, whose character is thus marked by every act which may define a Tyrant, is unfit to be the ruler of a free people.

Nor have We been wanting in attention to our British brethren. We have warned them from time to time of attempts by their legislature to extend an unwarrantable jurisdiction over us. We have reminded them of the circumstances of our emigration and settlement here. We have appealed to their native justice and magnanimity, and we have conjured them by the ties of our common kindred to disavow these usurpations, which would inevitably interrupt our connections and correspondence. They too have been deaf to the voice of justice and of consanguinity. We must, therefore, acquiesce in the necessity, which denounces our Separation, and hold them, as we hold the rest of mankind, Enemies in War, in Peace Friends.

We, therefore, the Representatives of the united States of America, in General Congress, Assembled, appealing to the Supreme Judge of the world for the rectitude of ou intentions, do, in the Name, and by Authority of the good People of these Colonies, solemnly publish and declare, That these United Colonies are, and of Right ought to be Free and Independent States; that they are Absolved from all Allegiance to the British Crown, and that all political connection between them and the State of Great Britain, is and ought to be totally dissolved; and that as Free and Independent States, they have full Power to levy War, conclude Peace, contract Alliances, establish Commerce, and to do al other Acts and Things which Independent States may of right do. And for the support of this Declaration, with a firm reliance on the Protection of Divine Providence, we mutually pledge to each other our Lives, our Fortunes and our sacred Honor.

Signers of the unanimous declaration. According to the Authenticated List printed by Order of Congress of January 18, 1877

JOHN HANCOCK.

NEW HAMPSHIRE
JOSIAH BARTLETT
WILLIAM WHIPPLE
MATTHEW THORNTON

MASSACHUSETTS-BAY
SAMUEL ADAMS
JOHN ADAMS
ROBERT TREAT PAINE
ELBRIDGE GERRY

RHODE ISLAND
STEPHEN HOPKINS
WILLIAM ELLERY

CONNECTICUT
ROGER SHERMAN
SAMUEL HUNTINGTON
WILLIAM WILLIAMS
OLIVER WOLCOTT

GEORGIA
BUTTON GWINNETT
LYMAN HALL
GEO. WALTON

MARYLAND
SAMUEL CHASE
WILLIAM PACA
THOMAS STONE
CHARLES CARROLL
OF CARROLLTON

VIRGINIA
GEORGE WYTHE
RICHARD HENRY LEE
THOMAS JEFFERSON
BENJAMIN HARRISON
THOMAS NELSON, JR.
FRANCIS LIGHTFOOT LEE
CARTER BRAXTON.

NEW YORK
WILLIAM FLOYD
PHILIP LIVINGSTON
FRANCIS LEWIS
LEWIS MORRIS

PENNSYLVANIA
ROBERT MORRIS
BENJAMIN RUSH
BENJAMIN FRANKLIN
JOHN MORTON
GEORGE CLYMER
JAMES SMITH
GEORGE TAYLOR
JAMES WILSON
GEORGE ROSS

DELAWARE
CAESAR RODNEY
GEORGE READ
THOMAS M'KEAN

NORTH CAROLINA
WILLIAM HOOPER
JOSEPH HEWES
JOHN PENN

SOUTH CAROLINA
EDWARD RUTLEDGE
THOMAS HEYWARD, JR.
THOMAS LYNCH, JR.
ARTHUR MIDDLETON

NEW JERSEY
RICHARD STOCKTON
JOHN WITHERSPOON
FRANCIS HOPKINS
JOHN HART
ABRAHAM CLARK

Constitution for the United States of America

We the People of the United States, in Order to form a more perfect Union, establish Justice, insure domestic Tranquility, provide for the common defence, promote the general Welfare, and secure the Blessings of Liberty to ourselves and our Posterity, do ordain and establish this Constitution for the United States of America.

Article. I.

Section. 1. All legislative Powers herein granted shall be vested in a Congress of the United States, which shall consist of a Senate and House of Representatives.

Section. 2. (01) The House of Representatives shall be composed of Members chosen every second Year by the People of the several States, and the Electors in each State shall have the Qualifications requisite for Electors of the most numerous Branch of the State Legislature.

(02) No Person shall be a Representative who shall not have attained to the Age of twenty five Years, and been seven Years a Citizen of the United States, and who shall not, when elected, be an Inhabitant of that State in which he shall be chosen.

(03) Representatives and direct Taxes shall be apportioned among the several States which may be included within this Union, according to their respective Numbers, which shall be determined by adding to the whole Number of free Persons, including those bound to Service for a Term of Years, and excluding Indians not taxed, three fifths of all other Persons. The actual Enumeration shall be made within three Years after the first Meeting of the Congress of the United States, and within every subsequent Term of ten Years, in such Manner as they shall by Law direct. The Number of Representatives shall not exceed one for every thirty Thousand, but each State shall have at Least one Representative; and until such enumeration shall be made, the State of New Hampshire shall be entitled to chuse three, Massachusetts eight, Rhode-Island and Providence Plantations one, Connecticut five, New-York six, New Jersey four, Pennsylvania eight, Delaware one, Maryland six, Virginia ten, North Carolina five, South Carolina five, and Georgia three.

(04) When vacancies happen in the Representation from any State, the Executive Authority thereof shall issue Writs of Election to fill such Vacancies.

(05) The House of Representatives shall chuse their Speaker and other Officers; and shall have the sole Power of Impeachment.

Section. 3. (01) The Senate of the United States shall be composed of two Senators from each State, chosen by the Legislature thereof, for six Years; and each Senator shall have one Vote.

(02) Immediately after they shall be assembled in Consequence of the first Election, they shall be divided as equally as may be into three Classes. The Seats of the Senators of the first Class shall be vacated at the Expiration of the second Year, of the second Class at the Expiration of the fourth Year, and of the third Class at the Expiration of the sixth Year, so that one third may be chosen every second Year; and if Vacancies happen by Resignation, or otherwise, during the Recess of the Legislature of any State, the Executive thereof may make temporary Appointments until the next Meeting of the Legislature, which shall then fill such Vacancies.

(03) No Person shall be a Senator who shall not have attained to the Age of thirty Years, and been nine Years a Citizen of the United States, and who shall not, when elected, be an Inhabitant of that State for which he shall be chosen.

(04) The Vice President of the United States shall be President of the Senate, but shall have no Vote, unless they be equally divided.

(05) The Senate shall chuse their other Officers, and also a President pro tempore, in the Absence of the Vice President, or when he shall exercise the Office of President of the United States.

(06) The Senate shall have the sole Power to try all Impeachments. When sitting for that Purpose, they shall be on Oath or Affirmation. When the President of the United States is tried, the Chief Justice shall preside: And no Person shall be convicted without the Concurrence of two thirds of the Members present.

(07) Judgment in Cases of Impeachment shall not extend further than to removal from Office, and disqualification to hold and enjoy any Office of honor, Trust or Profit under the United States: but the Party convicted shall nevertheless be liable and subject to Indictment, Trial, Judgment and Punishment, according to Law.

Section. 4. (01) The Times, Places and Manner of holding Elections for Senators and Representatives, shall be prescribed in each State by the Legislature thereof; but the Congress may at any time by Law make or alter such Regulations, except as to the Places of chusing Senators.

(02) The Congress shall assemble at least once in every Year, and such Meeting shall be on the first Monday in December [Modified by Amendment XX], unless they shall by Law appoint a different Day.

Section. 5. (01) Each House shall be the Judge of the Elections, Returns and Qualifications of its own Members, and a Majority of each shall constitute a Quorum to do Business; but a smaller Number may adjourn from day to day, and may be authorized to compel the Attendance of absent Members, in such Manner, and under such Penalties as each House may provide.

(02) Each House may determine the Rules of its Proceedings, punish its Members for disorderly Behaviour, and, with the Concurrence of two thirds, expel a Member.

(03) Each House shall keep a Journal of its Proceedings, and from time to time publish the same, excepting such Parts as may in their Judgment require Secrecy; and the Yeas and Nays of the Members of either House on any question shall, at the Desire of one fifth of those Present, be entered on the Journal.

(04) Neither House, during the Session of Congress, shall, without the Consent of the other, adjourn for more than three days, nor to any other Place than that in which the two Houses shall be sitting.

Section. 6. (01) The Senators and Representatives shall receive a Compensation for their Services, to be ascertained by Law, and paid out of the Treasury of the United States. They shall in all Cases, except Treason, Felony and Breach of the Peace, be privileged from Arrest during their Attendance at the Session of their respective Houses, and in going to and returning from the same; and for any Speech or Debate in either House, they shall not be questioned in any other Place.

(02) No Senator or Representative shall, during the Time for which he was elected, be appointed to any civil Office under the Authority of the United States, which shall have been created, or the Emoluments whereof shall have been encreased during such time; and no Person holding any Office under the United States, shall be a Member of either House during his Continuance in Office.

Section. 7. (01) All Bills for raising Revenue shall originate in the House of Representatives; but the Senate may propose or concur with Amendments as on other Bills.

(02) Every Bill which shall have passed the House of Representatives and the Senate, shall, before it become a Law, be presented to the President of the United States; If he approve he shall sign it, but if not he shall return it, with his Objections to that House in which it shall have originated, who shall enter the Objections at large on their Journal, and proceed to reconsider it. If after such Reconsideration two thirds of that House shall agree to pass the Bill, it shall be sent, together with the Objections, to the other House, by which it shall likewise be reconsidered, and if approved by two thirds of that House, it shall become a Law. But in all such Cases the Votes of both Houses shall be determined by yeas and Nays, and the Names of the Persons voting for and against the Bill shall be entered on the Journal of each House respectively. If any Bill shall not be returned by the President within ten Days (Sundays excepted) after it shall have been presented to him, the Same shall be a Law, in like Manner as if he had signed it, unless the Congress by their Adjournment prevent its Return, in which Case it shall not be a Law.

(03) Every Order, Resolution, or Vote to which the Concurrence of the Senate and House of Representatives may be necessary (except on a question of Adjournment) shall be presented to the President of the United States; and before the Same shall take Effect, shall be approved by him, or being disapproved by him, shall be repassed by two thirds of the Senate and House of Representatives, according to the Rules and Limitations prescribed in the Case of a Bill.

Section. 8. (01) The Congress shall have Power To lay and collect Taxes, Duties, Imposts and Excises, to pay the Debts and provide for the common Defence (sic) and general Welfare of the United States; but all Duties, Imposts and Excises shall be uniform throughout the United States;

(02) To borrow Money on the credit of the United States;

(03) To regulate Commerce with foreign Nations, and among the several States, and with the Indian Tribes;

(04) To establish an uniform Rule of Naturalization, and uniform Laws on the subject of Bankruptcies throughout the United States;

(05) To coin Money, regulate the Value thereof, and of foreign Coin, and fix the Standard of Weights and Measures;

(06) To provide for the Punishment of counterfeiting the Securities and current Coin of the United States;

(07) To establish Post Offices and post Roads;

(08) To promote the Progress of Science and useful Arts, by securing for limited Times to Authors and Inventors the exclusive Right to their respective Writings and Discoveries;

(09) To constitute Tribunals inferior to the supreme Court;

(10) To define and punish Piracies and Felonies committed on the high Seas, and Offences against the Law of Nations;

(11) To declare War, grant Letters of Marque and Reprisal, and make Rules concerning Captures on Land and Water;

(12) To raise and support Armies, but no Appropriation of Money to that Use shall be for a longer Term than two Years;

(13) To provide and maintain a Navy;

(14) To make Rules for the Government and Regulation of the land and naval Forces;

(15) To provide for calling forth the Militia to execute the Laws of the Union, suppress Insurrections and repel Invasions;

(16) To provide for organizing, arming, and disciplining, the Militia, and for governing such Part of them as may be employed in the Service of the United States, reserving to the States respectively, the Appointment of the Officers, and the Authority of training the Militia according to the discipline prescribed by Congress;

(17) To exercise exclusive Legislation in all Cases whatsoever, over such District (not exceeding ten Miles square) as may, by Cession of particular States, and the Acceptance of Congress, become the Seat of the Government of the United States, and to exercise like Authority over all Places purchased by the Consent of the Legislature of the State in which the Same shall be, for the Erection of Forts, Magazines, Arsenals, dock-Yards, and other needful Buildings; —And

(18) To make all Laws which shall be necessary and proper for carrying into Execution the foregoing Powers, and all other Powers vested by this Constitution in the Government of the United States, or in any Department or Officer thereof.

Section. 9. (01) The Migration or Importation of such Persons as any of the States now existing shall think proper to admit, shall not be prohibited by the Congress prior to the Year one thousand eight hundred and eight, but a Tax or duty may be imposed on such Importation, not exceeding ten dollars for each Person.

(02) The Privilege of the Writ of Habeas Corpus shall not be suspended, unless when in Cases of Rebellion or Invasion the public Safety may require it.

(03) No Bill of Attainder or ex post facto Law shall be passed.

(04) No Capitation, or other direct, Tax shall be laid, unless in Proportion to the Census or Enumeration herein before directed to be taken.

(05) No Tax or Duty shall be laid on Articles exported from any State.

(06) No Preference shall be given by any Regulation of Commerce or Revenue to the Ports of one State over those of another; nor shall Vessels bound to, or from, one State, be obliged to enter, clear, or pay Duties in another.

(07) No Money shall be drawn from the Treasury, but in Consequence of Appropriations made by Law; and a regular Statement and Account of the Receipts and Expenditures of all public Money shall be published from time to time.

(08) No Title of Nobility shall be granted by the United States: And no Person holding any Office of Profit or Trust under them, shall, without the Consent of the Congress, accept of any present, Emolument, Office, or Title, of any kind whatever, from any King, Prince, or foreign State.

Section. 10. (01) No State shall enter into any Treaty, Alliance, or Confederation; grant Letters of Marque and Reprisal; coin Money; emit Bills of Credit; make any Thing but gold and silver Coin a Tender in Payment of Debts; pass any Bill of Attainder, ex post facto Law, or Law impairing the Obligation of Contracts, or grant any Title of Nobility.

(02) No State shall, without the Consent of the Congress, lay any Imposts or Duties on Imports or Exports, except what may be absolutely necessary for executing its inspection Laws; and the net Produce of all Duties and Imposts, laid by any State on Imports or Exports, shall be for the Use of the Treasury of the United States; and all such Laws shall be subject to the Revision and Controul of the Congress.

(03) No State shall, without the Consent of Congress, lay any Duty of Tonnage, keep Troops, or Ships of War in time of Peace, enter into any Agreement or Compact with another State, or with a foreign Power, or engage in War, unless actually invaded, or in such imminent Danger as will not admit of delay.

Article. II.
Section. 1. (01) The executive Power shall be vested in a President of the United States of America. He shall hold his Office during the Term of four Years, and, together with the Vice President, chosen for the same Term, be elected, as follows:

(02) Each State shall appoint, in such Manner as the Legislature thereof may direct, a Number of Electors, equal to the whole Number of Senators and Representatives to which the State may be entitled in the Congress: but no Senator or Representative, or Person holding an Office of Trust or Profit under the United States, shall be appointed an Elector.

(03) The Electors shall meet in their respective States, and vote by Ballot for two Persons, of whom one at least shall not be an Inhabitant of the same State

with themselves. And they shall make a List of all the Persons voted for, and of the Number of Votes for each; which List they shall sign and certify, and transmit sealed to the Seat of the Government of the United States, directed to the President of the Senate. The President of the Senate shall, in the Presence of the Senate and House of Representatives, open all the Certificates, and the Votes shall then be counted. The Person having the greatest Number of Votes shall be the President, if such Number be a Majority of the whole Number of Electors appointed; and if there be more than one who have such Majority, and have an equal Number of Votes, then the House of Representatives shall immediately chuse by Ballot one of them for President; and if no Person have a Majority, then from the five highest on the List the said House shall in like Manner chuse the President. But in chusing the President, the Votes shall be taken by States, the Representation from each State having one Vote; a quorum for this Purpose shall consist of a Member or Members from two thirds of the States, and a Majority of all the States shall be necessary to a Choice. In every Case, after the Choice of the President, the Person having the greatest Number of Votes of the Electors shall be the Vice President. But if there should remain two or more who have equal Votes, the Senate shall chuse from them by Ballot the Vice President.

(04) The Congress may determine the Time of chusing the Electors, and the Day on which they shall give their Votes; which Day shall be the same throughout the United States.

(05) No Person except a natural born Citizen, or a Citizen of the United States, at the time of the Adoption of this Constitution, shall be eligible to the Office of President; neither shall any Person be eligible to that Office who shall not have attained to the Age of thirty five Years, and been fourteen Years a Resident within the United States.

(06) In Case of the Removal of the President from Office, or of his Death, Resignation, or Inability to discharge the Powers and Duties of the said Office, the Same shall devolve on the Vice President, and the Congress may by Law provide for the Case of Removal, Death, Resignation or Inability, both of the President and Vice President, declaring what Officer shall then act as President, and such Officer shall act accordingly, until the Disability be removed, or a President shall be elected.

(07) The President shall, at stated Times, receive for his Services, a Compensation, which shall neither be increased nor diminished during the Period for which he shall have been elected, and he shall not receive within that Period any other Emolument from the United States, or any of them.

(08) Before he enter on the Execution of his Office, he shall take the following Oath or Affirmation: — "I do solemnly swear (or affirm) that I will faithfully execute the Office of President of the United States, and will to the best of my Ability, preserve, protect and defend the Constitution of the United States."

Section. 2. (01) The President shall be Commander in Chief of the Army and Navy of the United States, and of the Militia of the several States, when called into the actual Service of the United States; he may require the Opinion, in writing, of the principal Officer in each of the executive Departments, upon any Subject relating to the Duties of their respective Offices, and he shall have Power to grant

Reprieves and Pardons for Offences against the United States, except in Cases of Impeachment.

(02) He shall have Power, by and with the Advice and Consent of the Senate, to make Treaties, provided two thirds of the Senators present concur; and he shall nominate, and by and with the Advice and Consent of the Senate, shall appoint Ambassadors, other public Ministers and Consuls, Judges of the supreme Court, and all other Officers of the United States, whose Appointments are not herein otherwise provided for, and which shall be established by Law: but the Congress may by Law vest the Appointment of such inferior Officers, as they think proper, in the President alone, in the Courts of Law, or in the Heads of Departments.

(03) The President shall have Power to fill up all Vacancies that may happen during the Recess of the Senate, by granting Commissions which shall expire at the End of their next Session.

Section. 3. He shall from time to time give to the Congress Information of the State of the Union, and recommend to their Consideration such Measures as he shall judge necessary and expedient; he may, on extraordinary Occasions, convene both Houses, or either of them, and in Case of Disagreement between them, with Respect to the Time of Adjournment, he may adjourn them to such Time as he shall think proper; he shall receive Ambassadors and other public Ministers; he shall take Care that the Laws be faithfully executed, and shall Commission all the Officers of the United States.

Section. 4. The President, Vice President and all civil Officers of the United States, shall be removed from Office on Impeachment for, and Conviction of, Treason, Bribery, or other high Crimes and Misdemeanors.

Article. III.

Section. 1. The judicial Power of the United States shall be vested in one supreme Court, and in such inferior Courts as the Congress may from time to time ordain and establish. The Judges, both of the supreme and inferior Courts, shall hold their Offices during good Behaviour, and shall, at stated Times, receive for their Services a Compensation, which shall not be diminished during their Continuance in Office.

Section. 2. (01) The judicial Power shall extend to all Cases, in Law and Equity, arising under this Constitution, the Laws of the United States, and Treaties made, or which shall be made, under their Authority; — to all Cases affecting Ambassadors, other public Ministers and Consuls; — to all Cases of admiralty and maritime Jurisdiction; — to Controversies to which the United States shall be a Party; — to Controversies between two or more States; — between a State and Citizens of another State; — between Citizens of different States; — between Citizens of the same State claiming Lands under Grants of different States, and between a State, or the Citizens thereof, and foreign States, Citizens or Subjects.

(02) In all Cases affecting Ambassadors, other public Ministers and Consuls, and those in which a State shall be Party, the supreme Court shall have original Jurisdiction. In all the other Cases before mentioned, the supreme Court shall have appellate Jurisdiction, both as to Law and Fact, with such Exceptions, and under such Regulations as the Congress shall make.

(03) The Trial of all Crimes, except in Cases of Impeachment, shall be by Jury; and such Trial shall be held in the State where the said Crimes shall have been committed; but when not committed within any State, the Trial shall be at such Place or Places as the Congress may by Law have directed.

Section. 3. (01) Treason against the United States shall consist only in levying War against them, or in adhering to their Enemies, giving them Aid and Comfort. No Person shall be convicted of Treason unless on the Testimony of two Witnesses to the same overt Act, or on Confession in open Court.

(02) The Congress shall have Power to declare the Punishment of Treason, but no Attainder of Treason shall work Corruption of Blood, or Forfeiture except during the Life of the Person attainted.

Article. IV.
Section. 1. Full Faith and Credit shall be given in each State to the public Acts, Records, and judicial Proceedings of every other State. And the Congress may by general Laws prescribe the Manner in which such Acts, Records and Proceedings shall be proved, and the Effect thereof.

Section. 2. (01) The Citizens of each State shall be entitled to all Privileges and Immunities of Citizens in the several States.

(02) A Person charged in any State with Treason, Felony, or other Crime, who shall flee from Justice, and be found in another State, shall on Demand of the executive Authority of the State from which he fled, be delivered up, to be removed to the State having Jurisdiction of the Crime.

(03) No Person held to Service or Labour in one State, under the Laws thereof, escaping into another, shall, in Consequence of any Law or Regulation therein, be discharged from such Service or Labour, but shall be delivered up on Claim of the Party to whom such Service or Labour may be due.

Section. 3. (01) New States may be admitted by the Congress into this Union; but no new State shall be formed or erected within the Jurisdiction of any other State; nor any State be formed by the Junction of two or more States, or Parts of States, without the Consent of the Legislatures of the States concerned as well as of the Congress.

(02) The Congress shall have Power to dispose of and make all needful Rules and Regulations respecting the Territory or other Property belonging to the United States; and nothing in this Constitution shall be so construed as to Prejudice any Claims of the United States, or of any particular State.

Section. 4. The United States shall guarantee to every State in this Union a Republican Form of Government, and shall protect each of them against Invasion; and on Application of the Legislature, or of the Executive (when the Legislature cannot be convened), against domestic Violence.

Article. V.
The Congress, whenever two thirds of both Houses shall deem it necessary, shall propose Amendments to this Constitution, or, on the Application of the Legislatures of two thirds of the several States, shall call a Convention for proposing Amendments, which, in either Case, shall be valid to all Intents and Purposes, as Part of this Constitution, when ratified by the Legislatures of three

fourths of the several States, or by Conventions in three fourths thereof, as the one or the other Mode of Ratification may be proposed by the Congress; Provided that no Amendment which may be made prior to the Year One thousand eight hundred and eight shall in any Manner affect the first and fourth Clauses in the Ninth Section of the first Article; and that no State, without its Consent, shall be deprived of its equal Suffrage in the Senate.

Article. VI.

(01) All Debts contracted and Engagements entered into, before the Adoption of this Constitution, shall be as valid against the United States under this Constitution, as under the Confederation.

(02) This Constitution, and the Laws of the United States which shall be made in Pursuance thereof; and all Treaties made, or which shall be made, under the Authority of the United States, shall be the supreme Law of the Land; and the Judges in every State shall be bound thereby, any Thing in the Constitution or Laws of any State to the Contrary notwithstanding.

(03) The Senators and Representatives before mentioned, and the Members of the several State Legislatures, and all executive and judicial Officers, both of the United States and of the several States, shall be bound by Oath or Affirmation, to support this Constitution; but no religious Test shall ever be required as a Qualification to any Office or public Trust under the United States.

Article. VII.

The Ratification of the Conventions of nine States, shall be sufficient for the Establishment of this Constitution between the States so ratifying the Same.

Preamble to the Bill of Rights

The conventions of a number of the states, having at the time of their adopting the Constitution, expressed a desire, in order to prevent misconstruction or abuse of its powers, that further declaratory and restrictive clauses should be added: And as extending the ground of public confidence in the government, will best insure the beneficent ends of its institution.

Bill of Rights

First Amendment
Congress shall make no law respecting an establishment of religion, or prohibiting the free exercise thereof; or abridging the freedom of speech, or of the press; or the right of the people peaceably to assemble, and to petition the Government for a redress of grievances.

Second Amendment
A well regulated Militia, being necessary to the security of a free State, the right of the people to keep and bear Arms, shall not be infringed.

Third Amendment
No Soldier shall, in time of peace be quartered in any house, without the consent of the Owner, nor in time of war, but in a manner to be prescribed by law.

Fourth Amendment
The right of the people to be secure in their persons, houses, papers, and effects, against unreasonable searches and seizures, shall not be violated, and no Warrants shall issue, but upon probable cause, supported by Oath or affirmation, and particularly describing the place to be searched, and the persons or things to be seized.

Fifth Amendment
No person shall be held to answer for a capital, or otherwise infamous crime, unless on a presentment or indictment of a Grand Jury, except in cases arising in the land or naval forces, or in the Militia, when in actual service in time of War or public danger; nor shall any person be subject for the same offence to be twice put in jeopardy of life or limb; nor shall be compelled in any criminal case to be a witness against himself, nor be deprived of life, liberty, or property, without due process of law; nor shall private property be taken for public use, without just compensation.

Sixth Amendment
In all criminal prosecutions, the accused shall enjoy the right to a speedy and public trial, by an impartial jury of the State and district wherein the crime shall

have been committed, which district shall have been previously ascertained by law, and to be informed of the nature and cause of the accusation; to be confronted with the witnesses against him; to have compulsory process for obtaining witnesses in his favor, and to have the Assistance of Counsel for his defence.

Seventh Amendment

In Suits at common law, where the value in controversy shall exceed twenty dollars, the right of trial by jury shall be preserved, and no fact tried by a jury, shall be otherwise re-examined in any Court of the United States, than according to the rules of the common law.

Eighth Amendment

Excessive bail shall not be required, nor excessive fines imposed, nor cruel and unusual punishments inflicted.

Ninth Amendment

The enumeration in the Constitution, of certain rights, shall not be construed to deny or disparage others retained by the people.

Tenth Amendment

The powers not delegated to the United States by the Constitution, nor prohibited by it to the States, are reserved to the States respectively, or to the people.

Additional Amendments to the Constitution

[Article. XI.][Proposed 1794; Ratified 1798]

The Judicial power of the United States shall not be construed to extend to any suit in law or equity, commenced or prosecuted against one of the United States by Citizens of another State, or by Citizens or Subjects of any Foreign State.

[Article. XII.][Proposed 1803; Ratified 1804]

The Electors shall meet in their respective states, and vote by ballot for President and Vice-President, one of whom, at least, shall not be an inhabitant of the same state with themselves; they shall name in their ballots the person voted for as President, and in distinct ballots the person voted for as Vice-President, and they shall make distinct lists of all persons voted for as President, and of all persons voted for as Vice-President, and of the number of votes for each, which lists they shall sign and certify, and transmit sealed to the seat of the government of the United States, directed to the President of the Senate; — The President of the Senate shall, in the presence of the Senate and House of Representatives, open all the certificates and the votes shall then be counted; — The person having the greatest number of votes for President, shall be the President, if such number be a majority of the whole number of Electors appointed; and if no person have such majority, then from the persons having the highest numbers not exceeding three on the list of those voted for as President, the House of Representatives shall choose immediately, by ballot, the President. But in choosing the President, the votes shall be taken by states, the representation from each state having one vote; a quorum for this purpose shall consist of a member or members from two-thirds of the states, and a majority of all the states shall be necessary to a choice. And if the House of Representatives shall not choose a President whenever the right of choice shall devolve upon them, before the fourth day of March next following, then the Vice-President shall act as President, as in the case of the death or other constitutional disability of the President. — The person having the greatest number of votes as Vice-President, shall be the Vice-President, if such number be a majority of the whole number of Electors appointed, and if no person have a majority, then from the two highest numbers on the list, the Senate shall choose the Vice-President; a quorum for the purpose shall consist of two-thirds of the whole number of Senators, and a majority of the whole number shall be necessary to a choice. But no person constitutionally ineligible to the office of President shall be eligible to that of Vice-President of the United States.

Article. XIII. [Proposed 1865; Ratified 1865]

Section. 1. Neither slavery nor involuntary servitude, except as a punishment for crime whereof the party shall have been duly convicted, shall exist within the United States, or any place subject to their jurisdiction.

Section. 2. Congress shall have power to enforce this article by appropriate legislation.

Article. XIV. [Proposed 1866; Ratified 1868]

Section. 1. All persons born or naturalized in the United States, and subject to the jurisdiction thereof, are citizens of the United States and of the State wherein they reside. No State shall make or enforce any law which shall abridge the privileges or immunities of citizens of the United States; nor shall any State deprive any person of life, liberty, or property, without due process of law; nor deny to any person within its jurisdiction the equal protection of the laws.

Section. 2. Representatives shall be apportioned among the several States according to their respective numbers, counting the whole number of persons in each State, excluding Indians not taxed. But when the right to vote at any election for the choice of electors for President and Vice President of the United States, Representatives in Congress, the Executive and Judicial officers of a State, or the members of the Legislature thereof, is denied to any of the male inhabitants of such State, being twenty-one years of age, and citizens of the United States, or in any way abridged, except for participation in rebellion, or other crime, the basis of representation therein shall be reduced in the proportion which the number of such male citizens shall bear to the whole number of male citizens twenty-one years of age in such State.

Section. 3. No person shall be a Senator or Representative in Congress, or elector of President and Vice President, or hold any office, civil or military, under the United States, or under any State, who, having previously taken an oath, as a member of Congress, or as an officer of the United States, or as a member of any State legislature, or as an executive or judicial officer of any State, to support the Constitution of the United States, shall have engaged in insurrection or rebellion against the same, or given aid or comfort to the enemies thereof. But Congress may by a vote of two-thirds of each House, remove such disability.

Section. 4. The validity of the public debt of the United States, authorized by law, including debts incurred for payment of pensions and bounties for services in suppressing insurrection or rebellion, shall not be questioned. But neither the United States nor any State shall assume or pay any debt or obligation incurred in aid of insurrection or rebellion against the United States, or any claim for the loss or emancipation of any slave; but all such debts, obligations and claims shall be held illegal and void.

Section. 5. The Congress shall have power to enforce, by appropriate legislation, the provisions of this article.

Article. XV. [Proposed 1869; Ratified 1870]

Section. 1. The right of citizens of the United States to vote shall not be denied or abridged by the United States or by any State on account of race, color, or previous condition of servitude.

Section. 2. The Congress shall have power to enforce this article by appropriate legislation.

Article. XVI. [Proposed 1909; Questionably Ratified 1913]

The Congress shall have power to lay and collect taxes on incomes, from whatever source derived, without apportionment among the several States, and without regard to any census or enumeration.

Article. XVII. [Proposed 1912; Ratified 1913]

The Senate of the United States shall be composed of two Senators from each State, elected by the people thereof, for six years; and each Senator shall have one vote. The electors in each State shall have the qualifications requisite for electors of the most numerous branch of the State legislatures.

When vacancies happen in the representation of any State in the Senate, the executive authority of such State shall issue writs of election to fill such vacancies: Provided, That the legislature of any State may empower the executive thereof to make temporary appointments until the people fill the vacancies by election as the legislature may direct.

This amendment shall not be so construed as to affect the election or term of any Senator chosen before it becomes valid as part of the Constitution.

Article. XVIII. [Proposed 1917; Ratified 1919; Repealed 1933]
(See Amendment XXI, Section 1)

Section. 1. After one year from the ratification of this article the manufacture, sale, or transportation of intoxicating liquors within, the importation thereof into, or the exportation thereof from the United States and all territory subject to the jurisdiction thereof for beverage purposes is hereby prohibited.

Section. 2. The Congress and the several States shall have concurrent power to enforce this article by appropriate legislation.

Section. 3. This article shall be inoperative unless it shall have been ratified as an amendment to the Constitution by the legislatures of the several States, as provided in the Constitution, within seven years from the date of the submission hereof to the States by the Congress.

Article. [XIX.] [Proposed 1919; Ratified 1920]

The right of citizens of the United States to vote shall not be denied or abridged by the United States or by any State on account of sex.

Congress shall have power to enforce this article by appropriate legislation.

Article. [XX.] [Proposed 1932; Ratified 1933]

Section. 1. The terms of the President and Vice President shall end at noon on the 20th day of January, and the terms of Senators and Representatives at noon on the 3d day of January, of the years in which such terms would have ended if this article had not been ratified; and the terms of their successors shall then begin.

Section. 2. The Congress shall assemble at least once in every year, and such meeting shall begin at noon on the 3d day of January, unless they shall by law appoint a different day.

Section. 3. If, at the time fixed for the beginning of the term of the President, the President elect shall have died, the Vice President elect shall become President. If a President shall not have been chosen before the time fixed for the beginning of his term, or if the President elect shall have failed to qualify, then the Vice President elect shall act as President until a President shall have qualified; and the Congress may by law provide for the case wherein neither a President elect nor a Vice President elect shall have qualified, declaring who shall then act as President, or the manner in which one who is to act shall be selected, and such person shall act accordingly until a President or Vice President shall have qualified.

Section. 4. The Congress may by law provide for the case of the death of any of the persons from whom the House of Representatives may choose a President whenever the right of choice shall have devolved upon them, and for the case of the death of any of the persons from whom the Senate may choose a Vice President whenever the right of choice shall have devolved upon them.

Section. 5. Sections 1 and 2 shall take effect on the 15th day of October following the ratification of this article.

Section. 6. This article shall be inoperative unless it shall have been ratified as an amendment to the Constitution by the legislatures of three-fourths of the several States within seven years from the date of its submission.

Article. [XXI.] [Proposed 1933; Ratified 1933]
Section. 1. The eighteenth article of amendment to the Constitution of the United States is hereby repealed.

Section. 2. The transportation or importation into any State, Territory, or possession of the United States for delivery or use therein of intoxicating liquors, in violation of the laws thereof, is hereby prohibited.

Section. 3. This article shall be inoperative unless it shall have been ratified as an amendment to the Constitution by conventions in the several States, as provided in the Constitution, within seven years from the date of the submission hereof to the States by the Congress.

Article. [XXII.] [Proposed 1947; Ratified 1951]
Section. 1. No person shall be elected to the office of the President more than twice, and no person who has held the office of President, or acted as President, for more than two years of a term to which some other person was elected President shall be elected to the office of the President more than once. But this Article shall not apply to any person holding the office of President when this Article was proposed by the Congress, and shall not prevent any person who may be holding the office of President, or acting as President, during the term within which this Article becomes operative from holding the office of President or acting as President during the remainder of such term.

Section. 2. This article shall be inoperative unless it shall have been ratified as an amendment to the Constitution by the legislatures of three-fourths of the several States within seven years from the date of its submission to the States by the Congress.

Article. [XXIII.] [Proposed 1960; Ratified 1961]
Section. 1. The District constituting the seat of Government of the United States shall appoint in such manner as the Congress may direct:

A number of electors of President and Vice President equal to the whole number of Senators and Representatives in Congress to which the District would be entitled if it were a State, but in no event more than the least populous State; they shall be in addition to those appointed by the States, but they shall be considered, for the purposes of the election of President and Vice President, to be electors appointed by a State; and they shall meet in the District and perform such duties as provided by the twelfth article of amendment.

Section. 2. The Congress shall have power to enforce this article by appropriate legislation.

Article. [XXIV.] [Proposed 1962; Ratified 1964]

Section. 1. The right of citizens of the United States to vote in any primary or other election for President or Vice President, for electors for President or Vice President, or for Senator or Representative in Congress, shall not be denied or abridged by the United States or any State by reason of failure to pay any poll tax or other tax.

Section. 2. The Congress shall have power to enforce this article by appropriate legislation.

Article. [XXV.] [Proposed 1965; Ratified 1967]

Section. 1. In case of the removal of the President from office or of his death or resignation, the Vice President shall become President.

Section. 2. Whenever there is a vacancy in the office of the Vice President, the President shall nominate a Vice President who shall take office upon confirmation by a majority vote of both Houses of Congress.

Section. 3. Whenever the President transmits to the President pro tempore of the Senate and the Speaker of the House of Representatives his written declaration that he is unable to discharge the powers and duties of his office, and until he transmits to them a written declaration to the contrary, such powers and duties shall be discharged by the Vice President as Acting President.

Section. 4. Whenever the Vice President and a majority of either the principal officers of the executive departments or of such other body as Congress may by law provide, transmit to the President pro tempore of the Senate and the Speaker of the House of Representatives their written declaration that the President is unable to discharge the powers and duties of his office, the Vice President shall immediately assume the powers and duties of the office as Acting President.

Thereafter, when the President transmits to the President pro tempore of the Senate and the Speaker of the House of Representatives his written declaration that no inability exists, he shall resume the powers and duties of his office unless the Vice President and a majority of either the principal officers of the executive department or of such other body as Congress may by law provide, transmit within four days to the President pro tempore of the Senate and the Speaker of the House of Representatives their written declaration that the President is unable to discharge the powers and duties of his office. Thereupon Congress shall decide the issue, assembling within forty-eight hours for that purpose if not in session. If the Congress, within twenty-one days after receipt of the latter written declaration, or, if Congress is not in session, within twenty-one days after Congress is required to assemble, determines by two-thirds vote of both Houses that the President is unable to discharge the powers and duties of his office, the Vice President shall continue to discharge the same as Acting President; otherwise, the President shall resume the powers and duties of his office.

Article. [XXVI.] [Proposed 1971; Ratified 1971]

Section. 1. The right of citizens of the United States, who are eighteen years of age or older, to vote shall not be denied or abridged by the United States or by any State on account of age.

Section. 2. The Congress shall have power to enforce this article by appropriate legislation.

Article. [XXVII.] [Proposed 1789; Ratified 1992;
Second of twelve Articles comprising the Bill of Rights]

No law, varying the compensation for the services of the Senators and Representatives, shall take effect, until an election of Representatives shall have intervened.

About the Author

Michael Badnarik was born and raised in Hammond, Indiana. Influenced by Jacques Cousteau, he learned to scuba dive and sail before learning how to skydive, windsurf, mountain climb and hang glide. Learning how to be a Presidential Candidate came later.

A former computer consultant who worked for Commonwealth Edison and Northrup, Michael began to study the Constitution in depth twenty years ago and soon realized, to his dismay, that many of the things our government does are actually unconstitutional. Determined to help all Americans understand and reclaim their political heritage and preserve their liberty, he developed a class to teach the Constitution, from which has come this book.

Though initially put-off by the "politics of politics," his greater understanding of the Constitution led him to the Libertarian Party and a renewed optimism for us all. After paying his dues in the field he became the Libertarian candidate for Texas House of Representatives in both 2000 and 2002.

Michael made his official bid for the Libertarian Party's presidential nomination on Presidents' Day 2003, and logged in over 25,000 miles of travel in the months leading up to the Party's National Convention in Atlanta and his victorious nomination the following May. His mother, Elaine Badnarik, made the nominating speech at the convention and was such a hit the Libertarian Party of Indiana made her their official candidate for Lt. Governor!

As the Libertarian Party's Presidential Candidate, Michael is traveling throughout the country in an attempt to help keep America great, while lighting the fires of liberty one heart and one mind at a time.